ORDINARY WOMEN – EXTRAORDINARY GOD

§

by Sandra Julian Barker

Other Books Available by Sandra Julian Barker

"Ivory & Ice" – a Christian novel
"The Frenchman" – a Christian novel
"Deadly Masquerade" – a novel
"The Formula" – a novel

"The Stuff of Nightmares" –
a Christian short story collection
"The House" – a novella

"A Trip to the Zoo" – a children's book

ORDINARY WOMEN – EXTRAORDINARY GOD

by Sandra Julian Barker

Copyright © 2015 Sandra Julian Barker
All Rights Reserved

Any unauthorized reprint or use of this material is prohibited without express written permission from the author and/or publisher.

Scripture quotations are from the New King James Version Bible, unless otherwise noted. Scripture taken from the New King James Version® Copyright © 1982 by Thomas Nelson. Used by permission. All rights reserved.

Quotations from *Jesus Calling* © 2008, Thomas Nelson, Inc., used by permission of author Sarah Young.

Cover photo by Sandra Julian Barker
Sculpture of a woman's pensive face and drooping wisteria vine at Balliol College in Oxford, England. Established in 1263, its one of the oldest of Oxford Universities.

Published by Joyful Writer Press,
Chesapeake, Virginia
ISBN 978-1519125774

This book is dedicated

To all my Soul Sisters -- what a joy
to share God's Word and His Spirit with you.
and
To our extraordinary God — Who is
the author of all of our stories
ↄ

Acknowledgment Page

I humbly thank God for laying this book upon my heart three years ago. It has been His book from the beginning and I believe He chose each story that has ended up on these pages. I feel privileged to have had a part in His work.

Thank you to my beloved family – my husband, three children and their spouses, and five grandchildren (with another on the way) and also my extended family – and to my precious Biltmore Baptist Church family – all of whom fill my life with love and support each and every day. I am so blessed!

Thank you to my daughter Sara, my sister Ava and friends Peggy Twiddy and Lou Ann Keiser for reading either portions or the entire manuscript and offering helpful suggestions and much-needed encouragement. Thank you to the many other sisters in Christ who offered words of encouragement and interest in these stories.

I offer an extra special thanks to Gretchen, Kyla, Judy, Sharon, Mary, Elizabeth, Eleanor, Lora, Sandy, Cindy, Shannon, and Lynda, precious Soul Sisters, and to Chip, a dear brother in Christ. I thank you for generously sharing your hearts and hurts in order to inspire and encourage all of us and to glorify the matchless name of our Father God. May Jesus Christ be praised!

ORDINARY WOMEN — EXTRAORDINARY GOD
Table of Contents

-- *Introduction* – God is With Us	8
-- *Habakkuk 3:17-19* – "Yet I Will Rejoice in the Lord"	...14
-- *Running with Horses* – Putting it into Perspective	...16
Ordinary Women - Past	...20
-- *Job's Wife* – Forgotten Suffering	...26
-- *Naomi* – from Bitter to Better	...32
Ordinary Women - Present	...38
-- *Gretchen's Story* – Yet, I will Praise Him	...42
-- *Kyla's Story* – God's Purpose	...48
-- *Judy's Story* – Preparing the Way	...56
-- *Sharon's Story* – Thankful Survivor	...64
-- *Mary's Story* – Overcoming the Overwhelming	...70
-- *Mama's Story* – Floodwaters and Grace	...74
-- *Sandra's Story* – God's Miracle Answer	...78
-- *Elizabeth's Story* – Identity in Christ	...82
-- *Eleanor's Story* – God Provides	...90
-- *Lora's Story* – Amazing Forgiveness	...94
-- *Sandy's Story* – God Knows the Future	..102
-- *Cindy's Story* – Pain, Loss & Healing	..118
-- *Shannon's Story* – God's Blessing – Above & Beyond	..128
-- *Lynda & Chip's Story* – Loss, Perseverance & a New Normal	..134
Finding Strength in God's Word	..141
-- *Sovereign God* – He is God Alone	..142
-- *Testing – One, Two, Three* – From Heaven's View	..148
-- *Fears* – Satan's Favorite Tool	..154
-- *Tears* – Fountains of Sadness & Gladness	..158
-- *His Grace is Sufficient* -- In His Time	..162
-- *Beauty from Ashes* -- Redemption & Restoration	..166
-- *A Blessing* – from God's Word	..172
-- *Salvation's Story* – How to be Saved	..174
-- *Author's Note*	..177
-- *Quotes from God's Extraordinary Word*	..178
-- *Songs in the Night*	..182
-- *Author page*	..185

~~ INTRODUCTION ~~

ORDINARY WOMEN AND
OUR EXTRAORDINARY GOD

In the midst of trouble - God is with us

"Be strong and of good courage, do not fear...for the Lord your God, He is the One who goes with you. He will not leave you nor forsake you" Deuteronomy 31:6

What do we do when life throws us a curve? How do we react? Does our view of God change?

How do you feel when your friend buys a new house, and you're still drowning in debt with foreclosure nipping at your heels? What do you say to your friend when she finds out she's pregnant, and you're fighting tears of childlessness? How do you cope with the loss of your beloved husband -- either through death, or sometimes worse -- infidelity? How do you walk through each new day when the doctor has painted the word "cancer" over your head? How do you handle a job loss, death of a loved one, financial ruin, betrayal, depression, pain and sickness? The list goes on and on ....

Sorrow, pain, heartbreak -- traumatic trials of every shape, size and color, are all part of life on this planet earth. How do we handle these events? How do we avoid bitterness poisoning our lives? How do we find our way back to the path of joy and peace after a season of sorrow, or even more of a challenge, how do we maintain joy and peace in the *midst* of a season of sorrow? And how do we cope when the issue will not be resolved on this side of heaven? Is it even possible?

~When the Ax Falls
My purpose for writing this book stems from my own search for an answer to these questions. I've had my share of struggles, but thus

far I've been spared the "biggies." I tend to be fearful that a major tragedy of some sort will happen in my life, and I don't know how I'll handle it. You know the old saying, "When will the ax fall?" I see others go through tragic and sorrowful circumstances, and I wonder how they do it. What can I learn from their experiences? What is the secret to surviving crushing loss or sorrowful circumstances, and still praising God?

If and when a severe tragedy strikes me or my family, I want to know that I'll be able to pass God's test and not let my banner of faith fall to the ground. When the floodwaters come, I want the assurance that I won't drown. I'm sure you want the same thing for your life.

"When my heart is overwhelmed; lead me to the
Rock that is higher than I" Psalm 61:2

Such questions brought me to a place of seeking out stories of ordinary women who have gone through the furnace of trial and have come out on the other side with barely a whiff of smoke clinging to their person. In one way or another, these ordinary women encountered our extraordinary God and, often through tears and struggle, let Him heal their wounds and bring them back to a safe place.

I want to know how they did it -- how they could let go of that sorrow and pain -- and heal. I want to know for myself, but I also want to discover the way for the many other sisters who also need to know how to walk this sometimes thorny path of life with a prayer on their lips and praise to God in their hearts -- even if the path is so dark we cannot see the next step in front of us.

~I Need Answers

Here are some questions we'd like answered: What can I say to someone to help ease the pain in a situation of extreme sorrow and pain? How do I answer the persistent cry of a friend with a hurting heart? Will I be able to cope if and when tragedy strikes in my own life? How do I keep the clawing pull of fear that something bad might happen at bay? How can I walk in peace in this world that is a jungle?

These are some of my questions -- and probably yours as well.

I'm at a loss for words when I try to comfort a friend during times of tragedy. I don't have an answer, and I don't want to belittle her situation with platitudes. All I can do is cry with her and wring my hands at her plight -- at least in my own strength and understanding.

I know that the only true answer we can ever find to these unexplainable pains and sorrow is found in the very real and living Words of our great Creator and loving Father. If we refuse to let His Words touch our hearts they will ring hollow and bounce off the shield of "self" we have erected and too often cling to.

I want to see how hurting women have let His loving Word permeate their souls -- Words that ring true, because they are true. His aiding and abiding Spirit can and will comfort in the midst of pain.

A myriad of questions may bubble up as we consider God's love -- why? How? When? Why again? We would not be human if these questions, full of anguish, did not arise in our hearts and minds. But God is patient and He understands that we are dust. He understands our anguish and lack. Did He not watch His own Son die a most painful death, yet not lift an all-powerful finger to ease His suffering?

Did God not watch His fresh, beautiful, innocent new creations succumb to the manipulative words of the evil one in a lovely garden He had created for them? His generous, loving heart must have burned with pain to see those two dearly beloved children sink their teeth into fruit that would ultimately destroy the world He had just created. He could have stopped it from happening, yet, in both situations, He did not stop the damage from occurring. He allowed the pain and sorrow to continue -- at least for a period, and always with a higher purpose.

That's what we so frequently fail to remember in the midst of our suffering -- that "*God's ways are not our ways,*" and that everything -- *everything* -- is for a purpose.

If we could see our suffering from Heaven's view, it would ease the pain, but since we can't do that, we must trust the One who can and cling to His promise that He will not put on us more than we can endure. And, that He does have a good outcome and a good purpose in the end.

~Women -- Together

When I shared my vision for this book with my daughter Sara, a young mother of two, she was excited. Here's what she said she hoped the book would be: "A chronicle of the Lord's power, forgiveness, redemption etc. As women we have to stick together and realize we are on the same team each trying to navigate through life. If we can talk about our struggles and guide each other to our compass which is the Lord and His Word, we can find our destination in Christ."

By the grace of God, I hope I have achieved that goal.

~Visiting Our Sisters

There you have it --- my purpose for this book -- to get a glimpse of God working through suffering, bringing beauty from ashes. By "visiting" with other sisters in Christ and hearing the stories of their encounters with our extraordinary God, we can share in those moments of both defeat and victory. I hope their experiences will strengthen us for the experiences that lie ahead of us. I also hope they will encourage those who still may be going through the "valley of the shadow" in one form or another.

The women (and one husband whose story was wrapped up in his wife's and too good to leave out) who share their stories in this book are just like you and me. Each of them would be the first to say there is no part of "super woman" that describes their lives. A few of the stories are taken from the Bible where we see sisters of the past who suffered just as we do today. Like us, these women were not super women, but were all sinners saved by grace and kept by the loving hand of our heavenly Father.

In addition to stories of women from the past and the present, I've included inspiring messages from God's Word to encourage your hearts and challenge you to see life from Heaven's view.

May God bless your heart, drawing you closer to His loving heart as you share the sorrows and struggles and victories of ordinary women just like you and me who have encountered the healing grace of our extraordinary God. *"If God be for us, who can be against us?"*

> *"'For My thoughts are not your thoughts, nor are your ways My ways,' says the Lord.*
> *For as the heavens are higher than the earth, so are My ways higher than your ways,*
> *and My thoughts than your thoughts"* Isaiah 55:8-9

~Note: I've always felt that photography can help give meaning and interest to a story. I've included courtesy photos with the women's stories, as well as photos taken by my husband Larry and myself in the other pieces. Hopefully, you'll agree that sometimes, "a picture is truly worth a thousand words."

Photo: Stained glass window in First Protestant Evangelical & Reformed Church (ca 1875), New Braunfels, Texas. SJB

HABAKKUK 3:17-19

I was reading through the book of Habakkuk one day when I discovered one of scripture's hidden gems. I refer to it as *hidden*, because I don't remember ever seeing or hearing about this verse before. As soon as I read the passage, I was stunned by its powerful message. I realized these were the verses that should form the backbone of this book about the stories of ordinary women who have encountered our extraordinary God.

> *"Though the fig tree may not blossom,*
> *nor fruit be on the vines;*
> *though the labor of the olive may fail,*
> *and the fields yield no food;*
> *though the flock may be cut off from the fold,*
> *and there be no herd in the stalls*
> *-- yet --*
> *I will rejoice in the Lord,*
> *I will joy in the God of my salvation.*
> *The Lord God is my strength;*
> *He will make my feet like deer's feet, and*
> *He will make me walk on my high hills"* 3:17-19

Bad things happen to good people every day of every week. We know this, but it's still a hard truth to accept when blows seem to come one after another with increasing frequency -- *yet* -- that word right there in the middle of a verse that begins with a litany of sorrowful events changes everything. It ends with an amazing joyful hallelujah and glorifying of our great God.

This then is what God desires from His children -- to praise Him in spite of our circumstances. It's easy to praise God when things are good, but when dark times engulf us and we still raise our voices in praise, that's when the greatest victory is won. That's where the true power of God and testimony of a Christian is seen by the world -- and by Satan and his cohorts as well. That's when the light of God shines through the darkness, filling the trusting heart with hope. And, that's when God is truly praised for Who He is -- not just for what He's done for us.

How amazing when we can say -- in spite of all the difficulty surrounding us -- "...*yet I will rejoice in the Lord, I will be joyful in God my Savior*" Habakkuk 3:18.

RUNNING WITH HORSES

If you have run with the footmen, and they have wearied you, then how can you contend with horses? And if in the land of peace in which you trusted, they wearied you, then how will you do in the floodplain of the Jordan? Jeremiah 12:5

When my dear pastor, T. M. Frye, quoted this verse at the beginning of his sermon one Sunday night, he immediately captured my attention. What a powerful message! And – like the verses in Habakkuk, I don't remember ever hearing or reading it before. I think it seems very appropriate for us to use at the beginning of this book – to help put things into perspective.

~Whining

Most of us have day to day problems, inconveniences and/or annoyances. I don't know about you, but I sometimes have a tendency to complain about these things (alright, I confess -- it's often more like full–blown *whining*). When things don't go according to plan or go smoothly, we are often unhappy campers.

There are also times we become weary with our day to day routine at the workplace, at school, or at home with family responsibilities. Such times often bring more whining.

Then there are times we become weary in the work of the Lord in our local church and Sunday School, or in whatever field of service to which God has called us. Sometimes we feel like we're swimming upstream and our labors are in vain because we see so little results. These are all among the "weary in well-doing" category and we're all guilty of it from time to time.

I would say that when circumstances in these various areas of life become what we might term "difficulties," they might constitute "running with the footmen."

Running with the footmen is something you and I can conceivably do. After all, footmen are people like you and me with two feet and the ability to run only so fast. It's not always easy, because they may be fast footmen, but with the help of God, we should be able to do the thing.

If we find ourselves whining about "*running with the footmen,*" we need to give ourselves a good shake, square our shoulders, and look up to the Lord for forgiveness, added strength and encouragement in the work He has given us to do. And be oh, so thankful that it's just footmen we're running with – because, it could be horses that we're contending with, and that is far more difficult.

God forbid I should complain about *anything* while I am dwelling in a land of peace. If I cannot rejoice in the Lord during a day that might hold some mild annoyances, unpleasant tasks and less than encouraging circumstances, what will I do when the Jordan floods its banks and I am inundated with floodwaters of difficulty, sorrow and/or pain?

~Horses are Fast!

Can you imagine running with a herd of horses? The average speed of a galloping horse is 30 mph, with the fastest recorded speed coming in at nearly 44 mph. A woman, on the other hand, might be able to sustain 8 mph running, with world class times of 14 mph for one mile. Either way, a woman's running speed is a far cry from the speed of a horse. That's no surprise – once again, it's an analogy that offers a contrast between mild difficulties compared to severe difficulties.

You stub your toe, that's a mild pain – you break your foot, that's a severe pain – you lose your leg, that's devastating and life-changing.

You get the picture. We need to beware of complaining when we're running with footmen, because there are a lot of Christians in this world who are trying to survive when forced to run with horses.

~Putting It in Perspective

I read in Sarah Young's *Jesus Calling* devotional book that if you "humbly bring Me [God] your prayers and petitions, your problems will pale when you view them in the Light of My Presence."

When I read that truth, it reminded me of sharing prayer requests in Bible study that week. I'd asked prayer for a dear sister who was not in our group. This sister had such a long list of really horrible things going on in her family that we all felt overwhelmed by her need.

One member of our group, Marlene, was so touched by the need of this sister, she said, "Well, I was going to ask for prayer, but after hearing this, I realize my life is good – I'm good."

Many times if we put our current needs into perspective compared with the needs of others, we'll say, "Hey, my life is good – I'm good."

Such an attitude will result in gratitude to God for all His blessings – and for realizing that "running with footmen" is not so bad after all.

~When Glory Shines Bright

As I talk with the women whose stories are shared in this book, I see that most of them are either currently running with horses, or have endured a run with them. Some of them have been chosen by God to run with the horses for the remainder of their earthly lives. Each of these women would be the first to tell us she could not keep up with the horses in her own strength – none of us can!

When the flood plains of Jordan overflow their banks and when we are forced to run with the horses, God has promised to be there to give ordinary women extraordinary strength and ability to keep up and run a supernatural race to His glory.

These women who are running with the horses – they're not whining or complaining. No doubt they have their low moments and even low weeks (who wouldn't??), but for the most part they are learning to trust and learning to let God do the running for them. This is when glory shines brightest – when life looks darkest. I am so encouraged by knowing it *can* be done.

This verse speaks to my heart as if God had reached down and wrote it on a note addressed to me. I have a feeling that many of you could say the same. If you, like me, find yourself living in the land of peace and running with footmen from time to time, let's put our circumstances into perspective. Instead of whining, let's be thankful for those footmen and pray that the horses keep their distance.

If the horses *do* come, I'm thankful God has promised He will give us strength to contend with them, but for now, thank you Lord for the footmen in my life.

"Let your light so shine before men, that they may see your good works and glorify your Father in heaven" Matthew 5:16

Photos: Horses - I spotted this beautiful herd of horses in a canyon at the Theodore Roosevelt National Park in Medora, North Dakota. SJB

Running -- Larry snapped the photo of me running between statues of Olympic runners (or footmen, we might call them) at the Olympic Village Museum in Colorado Springs, Colorado. It's interesting that I'm helping "carry a light." LNB

ORDINARY WOMEN –
of the past

"And the Lord God caused a deep sleep to fall on Adam, and he slept; and He took one of his ribs, and closed up the flesh in its place. Then the rib which the Lord God had taken from man He made into a woman..." Genesis 2:21-22

Throughout the Holy Bible we meet ordinary women, many of whom were called upon to accomplish extraordinary tasks. We have a goodly heritage from these Sisters of the past. Let's briefly look at a few of their stories.

~Deborah, Judge in Israel

We look at women like Deborah who was a judge in Israel at a time when women were still in the shadows of leadership. Yet, this woman went out as a leader of an army of 10,000 men and they defeated a far greater number of enemy. Her victory song is found in Judges 5, and ends with these words, *"Thus let all Your enemies perish, O Lord! But let those who love Him be like the sun when it comes out in full strength."*

Question: How does an ordinary woman like Deborah go from being a homemaker and the wife of Lapidoth to becoming the Judge of Israel and leader of an army?

Answer: She puts her faith in an extraordinary God and He does not fail her.

Deborah begins her song of victory, saying, *"I will sing praise to the Lord God of Israel. Lord, when You went out...."* Deborah is well-aware that it was God who went out before her and by His power the battle was won.

A verse in Zechariah 4:6 says it well, *"...Not by might nor by power, but by My Spirit, says the LORD of hosts."*

~Jochebed, Mother of Moses

How about an ordinary mother with two young children and a newborn baby? The family were Hebrews in bondage in ancient Egypt.

Question: How could such a woman possibly make an everlasting mark on this world?

Answer: She puts her faith in an extraordinary God and He does not fail her.

Exodus 2:1-10 tells the vivid story of Jochebed, a mother intent on saving her beautiful baby son from murderous intentions of an Egyptian Pharaoh. Every child who attends Sunday School hears the story of baby Moses floating in his little basket, rescued by an Egyptian princess, and raised as a prince in the palace.

Here, we consider his mother and her integral part in the story.

It was this young mother who took the reins to save the life of her baby son from certain death. God gave her the wisdom and courage to make this incredible effort in the face of much danger. With little thought for her own safety, but overpowering Mother-love filling her heart, she prepared a waterproof basket, tucked her precious baby boy deep inside, and anchored the vessel among thick reeds growing along the shallows of the Nile River. She then instructed her daughter Miriam (perhaps seven or eight years old) to keep watch over her little brother from a safe distance.

Scripture doesn't indicate how many days may have passed before the Egyptian Princess discovered the baby. As children hearing the story, we imagine it all happening quickly – within hours – and perhaps it did. But, we don't know how many days, or even weeks, Jochebed may have hidden her child, fearful that at any moment he might be discovered by enemy soldiers – or hungry crocodiles that infested the Nile.

If a period of time elapsed, she would also need to find opportunities to feed and change the baby throughout the day. How would she accomplish these necessary acts safely? What would she do when the baby became too old to quietly bob up and down in a basket all day? Did she have a long-term plan or was she winging it day by day?

This was not an easy task the young mother undertook, but as Hebrews 11:23 reminds us, she had faith in a God she believed was stronger than the king's command and God's power overcame her fear.

Of course, we know how the story ends. The Princess finds the baby, and immediately falls in love with this beautiful little boy. As God planned, Miriam comes forward and offers to find a wet nurse to suckle the baby. Thereby, his own mother Jochebed is able to safely raise him for the first few years of his life. She is able to continue nursing him without so much as a missed feeding, to hold him in her arms, and love him and teach him from God's Word – with no fear of the enemy soldiers.

Jochebed could never have imagined such a good ending to her story, but God had this amazing plan in place from the beginning.

Once Moses was old enough to be weaned (possibly as old as three or four years in ancient times), he was taken to the palace, his mother kissed him good-bye, and she may never have seen him again. We don't know, because scripture gives no indication and makes no further reference of his mother.

This was a bittersweet "happy ending" that was probably a hard conclusion for a mother to endure. In spite of the sadness of her empty arms, I hope that Jochebed remembered the words of Joseph, a Hebrew who not too many years earlier had been a great ruler in Egypt. Joseph said, *"...you meant evil against me, but God meant it for good, in order to bring it about as it is this day, to save many people alive"* Genesis 50:20.

And so it would be – unbeknownst to this mother, the child she risked her life to save would one day be used by God *"to save many people alive"* – in fact, the entire nation of Israel!

Her baby boy that she laid her life on the line to save, would be so honored of God, it would be written: *"But since then there has not arisen in Israel a prophet like Moses, whom the Lord knew face to face"* Deuteronomy 34:10.

~Rahab, the Gentile Convert

Here was a woman who had a lot of baggage to overcome in her effort to find redemption and serve God. This young woman was not only a heathen in an enemy city, but she was a harlot, considered a shameful, sinful lifestyle.

Question: How could such a woman ever hope to find salvation from both sin and destruction?

Answer: She puts her faith in an extraordinary God and He does not fail her.

We don't know the circumstances behind this woman's choice of occupation. Perhaps it was not so much a choice, as a necessity. This was the woman, however, that God chose to have a hand in saving His people. And as a result of her choice to help the spies, she and her family were spared from the destruction of the city.

Long before the Israelites neared Jericho, our sovereign God led this woman Rahab to move into a humble dwelling located between the wide city walls, with a window overlooking the land outside the walls. It would be the perfect place for Jewish spies to someday hide and escape, and for a scarlet cord to one day hang from a window and be seen by an invading army.

When news of Israelite victories reached the city of Jericho, its inhabitants melted with fear. Rahab's heart was touched by almighty God and she believed in Him, saying, *"...for the LORD your God, He is God in heaven above and on earth beneath"* Joshua 2:11.

Not only did Rahab have this new faith in God, she also had street-smarts and bravery (certainly gifts from God as well). She offered to help the Jewish spies evade capture and escape. She wisely obtained their promise to spare she and her family when the city was captured. This ancient sister who did not let her sordid past inhibit her shining future is listed in the Hebrews Hall of Fame: *"By faith the harlot Rahab did not perish with those who did not believe, when she had received the spies with peace"* 11:31.

As a result of her faith and bold actions, Rahab, a Gentile and former prostitute, is listed in the lineage of our Lord and Savior, Jesus Christ. You go, girl!

~Our Ancient Sisters
In addition to these brief stories of Deborah, Jochebed and Rahab, we'll look more closely into the lives of two other of our ancient sisters. We'll take a closer look at Job's Wife – a woman who doesn't even rate her name being recorded, yet suffered indescribable tragedy nearly as great as that of her husband. Then, we have Naomi, whose great loss resulted in bitterness that turned to blessing when God worked "all things for good" in her life.

> *"...For He Himself has said, 'I will never leave you nor forsake you.' So we may boldly say: 'The Lord is my helper; I will not fear. What can man do to me?'"*
> Hebrews 13:5-6

-Photo: Stained glass of Moses as baby in a church in Stow-on-the-Wold, England.
SJB

JOB'S WIFE

We don't even know her name. She's simply referred to as "Job's wife." On top of that, the two references to Job's wife in all of scripture are distinctly negative:

> "Then his wife said to him, 'Do you still hold fast to
> your integrity? Curse God and die!'"
> Job responds, "You speak as one of the foolish women speaks.
> Shall we indeed accept good from God and
> shall we not accept adversity?" 2:9-10.
> Then, in 19:17, Job makes a telling remark,
> "My breath is offensive to my wife."

It appears that Job's wife threw a low blow to her husband when he was already down – not a nice thing to do. Because of her negative behavior in that first moment, we tend to judge her badly, yet how often have we considered her plight in all this tragedy?

The book is about Job's righteousness in the face of tragedy and loss, and about God's sovereignty and plan for each person. There is much to learn from the riches tucked away in this ancient book. Broad strokes of deep truth brushed across the masterpiece of the book of Job tend to overshadow that subtle little dab of paint representing Job's wife.

Let's take a look at this woman who lived thousands of years ago, and see the similarities of her behavior and outlook on life with our present-day outlook.

~Sudden Reversal of Life as She Knew It

Here was a woman married to a wealthy man. She was probably a "Lady of the Manor" with fine clothes, servants to make her life easier and perhaps a high place in the society of her day. Throughout her perhaps thirty or so years of marriage to a fine man, her life had been blessed with smooth sailing – hardly a ripple to mar the sunny horizon of her days. We can surmise this because Job 1:10

tells how God had made *"a hedge around Job, around his household, and around all that he had on every side and blessed the work of his hands."*

Not only was she living the good life, she had seven grown sons and three daughters. She probably loved her children dearly, and enjoyed visiting with them. Perhaps she was even helping them plan an upcoming wedding or two. I can imagine she was already dreaming of grandchildren.

Then, in what amounted to one fell swoop, it felt like *everything* she held dear was taken away from her. Their vast flocks were stolen and their servants killed, but the worst tragedy for a mother is the loss of her children. Imagine losing all ten of your children in one sudden storm. Stop for a minute and let the enormity of that devastating tragedy become more than a simple sentence written on the page. I weep at the horror of seeing ten coffins with the broken remains of her beautiful beloved children within -- of knowing that not even one child was left to bring comfort to her grieving heart.

My heart breaks for this woman and the desolation she would have felt at such an incredible loss.

We all look at Job and his loss and cry in sympathy for him (after all, he is the main earthly character of the book), but I don't hear any sympathy for this woman's loss. The only thing we hear about her is condemnation for her thoughtless, hurtful words to Job.

Does anyone else feel like saying, "Hey, let's give the woman a break? She was in intense pain and her thoughtless comments may have been just that – words without thought, dripping in pain and anguish." I don't want to excuse this woman -- or to judge her -- that is definitely up to God, but I do want to try to learn something from her part in this ageless story.

The question is – what can we learn from her brief appearance in this tragedy?

~When Sorrow Strikes

Truths can seem like platitudes when you're in the depths of despair. If this woman's friends were anything like Job's three "friends," the words they intended for comfort fell flat and even burst like fiery darts against her unspeakable pain. Even verses of scripture meant to soothe can, in some cases, have the opposite affect and inflame a raw, hurting heart. There is a time for *words* of comfort and there is a time for *tearful hugs* of comfort that offer an unspoken message of sharing in your friend's grief.

~Guard Your Tongue

One of the important lessons we can learn from Job's wife's response is to be careful what words we speak. As women, we tend to have a need to vent – kind of like steam escaping from a safety valve to relieve and release harmful pressure. The trouble is, that steam can inflict painful burns.

In Job's wife's case, she really let the sparks fly! She did not mince words. She burned her husband with her words and there they are for all the world to see through all generations. What if some of the words you've spoken in rash moments were written down for all the world to see through all generations? Can't you imagine Job's wife looking down through the ages and wishing she'd just bitten her tongue in that moment?

David knew the answer to our need to vent and he addressed it numerous times in the Psalms. In chapter 142, he speaks of crying out to the Lord and said, *"I pour out my complaint before Him; I declare before Him my trouble."*

There we have the key to safely venting. Venting to the Lord is the best release for pressures that build in our hearts and minds. When we pour out our anguish to Him, He understands and His "invisible skin" doesn't burn. The additional benefits are that He provides comfort and replaces pain with peace – and – we don't have to worry about hurt feelings or our words being repeated to others.

Have you ever "told someone off" and wished later you'd kept your mouth shut? Have you ever repeated a story about someone or a secret you'd been told and been sorry you'd passed it on? Can you think of a situation when you should have kept your mouth shut and poured out feelings of frustration or hurt to God? It happens to all of us.

As James so succinctly put it, *"Even so the tongue is a little member and boasts great things. See how great a forest a little fire kindles! And the tongue is a fire, a world of iniquity. The tongue is so set among our members that it defiles the whole body, and sets on fire the course of nature; and it is set on fire by hell"* 3:5-6.

There is a way to "vent" to God about your pain and anguish without sinning. Sadly, I believe Job's wife did sin when she went so far as to say, *"Curse God and die!"* Let's be careful not to go so far.

Once again we use David as our example when he wrote, *"Give ear to my voice when I cry out to You. Let my prayer be set before You as incense...Set a guard, O Lord, over my mouth; keep watch over the door of my lips. Do not incline my heart to any evil thing..."* 141:1-3.

~Pain All Around

Over the years when we watch people endure trials and tragedy (or we endure them ourselves), we often say, "Well, at least it wasn't as bad as what Job went through." I don't know if any human has ever suffered to the extent that Job suffered – except for Job's wife. She shared in all of his pain except for his physical infirmity and even then, seeing him in pain probably hurt her as well.

On top of that, as the situation improved, she probably had more than a little guilt to deal with when she realized she'd failed to stand true to God during their period of adversity. A spotlight is shone on this woman's sin, while the extent of her suffering and agony is essentially ignored.

~How Did It End?

An interesting note is the fact that the mention of "Job's wife" doesn't appear anywhere else in the entire 42 chapters of the book. Even at the end when Job has been restored to his former health and glory, twice as rich as before, there is no mention of this woman.

Scripture tells us that he had a big party with all of his brothers and sisters and acquaintances, but again no wife is listed.

Then there's the part where God blesses Job with seven more sons and three more daughters. Scripture says, *"In all the land were found no women so beautiful as the daughters of Job; and their father gave them an inheritance among their brothers"* 42:15.

I've often wondered, who gave birth to these ten children? Was it the woman who'd already given birth to ten children and watched them grow to adulthood and die – did that same woman give birth to ten more children?

Did she and Job have a reconciliation after the harsh words she threw at him in chapter two and the way she disdained him in chapter nineteen?

Although we don't have a definitive answer to these questions, there is no mention of another wife. I can only hope that Job's wife repented of her sinful behavior and turned to God for comfort during that dreadfully sad time in her life. I hope she was able to live the promise of God: *"...weeping may remain for a night, but rejoicing comes in the morning"* Psalm 30:5.

It would be an unbelievably hard thing to endure all the loss Job's wife suffered. I can well imagine that all of us would go through a time of overwhelming grief that would pitch us into a "slough of despond" as the Pilgrim described it.

We are so blessed to have forms of comfort that Job's wife did not have available to her – the Holy Bible which is the written Word of the Most High God to comfort and guide us, and the Holy Spirit Himself as our indwelling comforter to draw us to the very throne of our Father. When Jesus Christ died and became our Savior, the veil separating us from the Holy of Holies was torn from top to bottom by the hand of God. We now have the amazing privilege of communing directly with Almighty God.

Although Job's wife lived during Old Testament times, God has always been a loving God of forgiveness who understands that His children are "dust." Over and over in scripture, the Lord urges His children to repent of sins because He is eager to forgive and pretty much forget, as evidenced in the verses in Psalm 103: *"For as high as the heavens are above the earth, so great is His love for those who fear*

Him; as far as the east is from the west, so far has He removed our transgressions from us" 11-12.

None of us know the details of what transpired in that long-ago situation in the land of Uz, but I'd like to think that Job's wife repented of her sins, got her act together and joined in the family rejoicing when God once again brought blessing into Job's life.

Scripture tells us that Job lived 140 years after these things happened and *"saw his children and grandchildren for four generations."* I hope the original "Job's wife" was there to snuggle and love on those precious children and grandchildren and to grow old with the husband of her youth.

Our extraordinary God is the gracious Author of second chances.

Photo: Statue of a mourning woman on a grave in Santa Maria Magdalena de Pazzis Cemetery in San Juan, Puerto Rico. SJB

NAOMI – FROM BITTER TO BETTER

"..Do not call me Naomi, call me Mara, for the Almighty has dealt very bitterly with me" Ruth 1:20

Naomi's name is pinned to the beginning of the book as well as the ending and all points in between, yet another holds the title of the little four chapter book of Ruth. Many consider the main character in the book to be Ruth, but it looks to me like Naomi is behind the scenes calling the shots and Ruth is just following her direction. I'm not a Biblical scholar, but I'm just saying ---

~Naomi's Story

When our story begins, Naomi is a young mother with a husband and two sons. She and her family travel from their home in Bethlehem into the country of Moab because of a famine in the land of Judah. After a period of time, her husband Elimelech dies, and she is left in a foreign land with her two boys.

We're not told how many years transpired for these earlier events. Scripture simply says of her sons, *"Now they took wives of the women of Moab: the name of the one was Orpah, and the name of the other Ruth. And they dwelt there about ten years"* Ruth 1:4.

Here, we're finally given a period of time. It appears that after the young men married, they remained in Moab for another ten years – plenty of time for Naomi to form a strong bond with these two young women. In those days, wives often moved into the homes of their husband's family. It's likely that Naomi would have taught the women what she knew of cooking and keeping house – and I would imagine that she also told them of God and His history with the Jewish people as well.

At this point, I don't believe Naomi was bitter about her situation. She still had two sons and their wives, and the hope of grandchildren to fill her arms. Moab wasn't Bethlehem, but at least she was surrounded by her family. She was probably content.

Then, the unthinkable happened. Both sons died. Don't you wish scripture gave a bit more detail when it comes to these stories? I'd like to know what they died of and how close together were their deaths. When I read the meaning of the two son's names, I'm not surprised at their early demise. Their names were: Mahlon, meaning "sickly," and Chilion, meaning "failing." Perhaps she should have given them different names...

It would have been a terrible blow to a widowed mother to suddenly lose her only two sons. And to top it all off, she was living in a foreign land away from her ancestral home and old friends. This is where the bitterness begins to creep in, when Naomi says to the two women, *"....the hand of the Lord has gone out against me"* 1:13.

By this time the famine in Judah was past. Naomi felt it was time for her to return to her own people. She released both of her daughters-in-law from her care and told them to go out and find other husbands for themselves. Although she wept at their parting, Orpah returned to her family and in so doing – to her gods. Ruth, however, refused to leave Naomi and vowed to stay with her – to align herself with Naomi, her home, her people and, most importantly -- her God.

I believe that Ruth had seen something in Naomi's faith over the years – something that spoke to a need deep within her own heart. God was calling this young woman to Himself and she obediently answered His call.

~Back Home to Bethlehem
Naomi and Ruth walked along dusty roads together for perhaps a week before arriving at the village of Bethlehem where Naomi had previously lived. When her old friends greeted her, Naomi said to them, *"Do not call me Naomi [meaning "pleasant"], call me Mara [meaning "bitter"], for the Almighty has dealt very bitterly with me. I went out full, and the Lord has brought me home again empty...the Almighty has afflicted me"* Ruth 1:20-21.

At least Naomi was being honest and admitting everything was not hunky-dory. She'd had a tough time of it and was coming back empty-handed – but, regardless of all these set-backs, the Lord had brought her back home again.

The fact that Naomi called herself Bitter doesn't necessarily mean she was bitter against God, but rather that she was bitter about her circumstances. She felt like the hand of God had knocked her down, so to speak. What she didn't realize and what we've seen transpire in the book of Job, is that God doesn't knock people down. He does, however, sometimes allow Satan to knock people down, but only because He has a purpose for the hardship and in the end, it is His plan to pick them up again.

~Bitter to Better

There's so much more going on behind the scenes of our ups and downs in life – things that we may never know about on this earth, but things that have value and purpose in God's sovereign plan. It's easy to lose sight of that truth and grow bitter ourselves, but bitterness is a poison and only brings pain.

Naomi didn't realize it at the time, but her bitter would soon get so much better. By the end of the fourth chapter, Naomi is seen joyously cradling a baby boy in her arms and her friends are speaking of the baby, saying to her, *"Blessed be the Lord...and may he* [the baby] *be to you a restorer of life and nourisher of your old age; for your daughter-in-law, who loves you, who is better to you than seven sons, has borne him...There is a son born to Naomi..."* Ruth 4.

The baby's name was Obed -- *"Obed begot Jesse, and Jesse begot David"* Ruth 4:22.

Obed's grandson David said it well, *"Weeping may endure for a night, but joy comes in the morning"* Psalm 30:5.

~My Story

Praise God, I am not a person who normally harbors bitterness. Only twice in my life have I experienced the pain and poison of bitterness in my heart. It was a learning experience, but it was also horrible and I hope I never have to endure feeling bitterness again!

In Beth Moore's devotional book, *Whispers of Hope*, she writes, "Prayer for those who have hurt us is not just for their sakes -- it's for OURS!" That's especially true if the other person doesn't even realize or acknowledge there's a problem, as is sometimes the case. By the power of the Holy Spirit, we can forgive a person for something that person was not even asking forgiveness for, nor were they apparently aware there was even an issue. The burden that is lifted by that simple internal act is indescribable.

The first time I ever experienced bitterness was over twenty years ago and it lasted for less than two weeks. I'm not sure how long it would have lasted if my dear Christian friend who was involved in the hurtful issue had not come to me and wisely said, "You are dear to me. Please, let us agree to disagree on this matter." God was in that moment and He knew those were the exact words I needed to hear to let go of the caustic bitterness that had grown in a very short time. It was as if a balloon in my heart had filled with toxic air and with those words and the power of the Holy Spirit working, the Lord pricked that balloon of bitterness and it deflated as if it had never even been there. The immediate and all-encompassing healing was miraculous and there is no shred of ill-will to this day. God replaced it with an even deeper friendship than we'd shared before.

Surprisingly, that was the first time I'd ever experienced bitterness. I believe God allowed me to go through that intensely painful situation to teach me what bitterness feels like and how it can harm a relationship – and how quickly it can form. Looking back, I believe that Satan's henchmen threw the poison blanket of bitterness over me and I hugged it to myself because, at the time, it felt right. The powers of darkness meant it for evil, but as Joseph once wisely said, *"God meant it for good..."* Genesis 50:20. God wanted me to learn a very important lesson and I thank Him for it.

As in all things, He is the Potter, I am the clay. He has a purpose for everything He allows to come into our lives. That painful situation is not one I would have chosen, but now I thank God for it and I love the fact that the demon's plans were foiled again. I'm very happy that I was bitter, but now I'm better – praise God!

~The Baggage of Bitterness?

There are so many reasons people carry bitterness within their souls. A hurt in childhood, adolescents, college, marriage, family, co-workers, church – you name it, there are big and small hurts that have happened to all of us. But what is it that makes a *hurt* transform into *bitterness*?

A young woman shared with me about the bitterness she'd carried for abuse she received as a child, and how it colored her outlook on life and her relationship with others in negative ways. She says she kept the secret from her family and her husband, and felt like she was living a lie for many years. Only recently was she able to let her bitterness go.

Another woman is bitter toward God for a loss in her life that she considers unfair and she just can't get past it. The bitterness is sucking peace and joy from her and it too colors her outlook on life.

Why is it so hard to let go of bitterness?

I think that often people can't let go of bitterness because they feel like it means they're accepting that what was done to them is okay, therefore, there's no way they can let it go. By holding onto it, they're making sure it's never accepted as "okay."

Letting go of bitterness doesn't mean you're saying "it's okay." Definitely not! Rather, it means that through the power of Jesus, you're forgiving someone who may not even have asked for forgiveness, or you're agreeing to disagree with someone, or you're accepting the fact that God does know best, or whatever it is that you need to do. Ask God to help you get through the process, and as that oh-so popular song says, "Let it go, let it go…"

Carrying bitterness in your heart is sort of like carrying bulky luggage around all the time. It's a heavy burden. It's painful. It's not healthy and – it's not of the Lord. The supernatural healing offered by our extraordinary Father is such a beautiful thing!

We desperately need to let go of the baggage of bitterness in our hearts?

Here are a few admonitions on the subject from our Father's Word: *"If it is possible, as much as depends on you, live peaceably with all men"* – and I might add, all women too – Romans 12:18.

"For if you forgive men their trespasses, Your heavenly Father will also forgive you" Matthew 5:14.

"Let all bitterness and wrath and anger and clamor and slander be put away from you, along with all malice. Be kind to one another, tenderhearted, forgiving one another, as God in Christ forgave you" Ephesians 4:31-32.

ORDINARY WOMEN –
of the Present

"Jesus Christ is the same yesterday, today, and forever"
Hebrews 13:8

One thing I've learned about life on this ole earth is that we have not changed all that much from the day God created us thousands of years ago. Ordinary women today are still called upon to accomplish extraordinary tasks – by the power of the Holy Spirit that works within the hearts of those of us who are saved.

This book contains the stories of women (and one man) of today – ordinary women like you and me who have experienced testing and tragedy, sorrow and pain. Each of them have either come through or are still going through challenging, heartbreaking experiences with God's praises on their lips and His love in their hearts. These are women who struggle and question and hurt just like you and I. Yet, in spite of it all, their testimonies exhibit a living faith and shine a light on the grace of our loving Father.

Theirs are stories that stir the soul, much like those of our ancient sisters - women throughout history who stood in the power of our extraordinary God, with tears in their eyes and a tremulous smile on their lips, perhaps whispering words similar to that dear, old song, "For I know whom I have believed and am persuaded that He is able, to keep that which I've committed unto Him against that day" (hymn lyrics by Daniel W. Whittle).

I'd like to introduce you to the present day Sisters in Christ we will be visiting in this book. These are women who do not seek the limelight nor do they feel they are in any way special among women. When I asked them to share their stories with us, each of them at one point expressed the sentiment written to me by one sister, who said, "I do not feel in any way amazing except in ways that God has blessed me. If that brings glory to Him, I am for it."

I wish to thank each of the women who so generously shared the stories of tragic and difficult times in their lives. I feel tremendously humbled to be a part of this work. It is my hope that, not only have these Sisters been blessed by sharing their stories, but that each of us will receive blessing and a renewed vision by reading what they have shared with us.

Each woman tells her story in her own unique way. Formats will vary, but faith in God ultimately shines through the darkness. Each woman's story reveals a facet of Holy God's plan for our lives.

Without further ado, let me introduce you to these lovely – and extraordinary women:

--Gretchen: At 42 years old, she'd made peace with the fact she would never have a child. She was content serving God in children's ministry. Then, a miracle occurred and she discovered she was pregnant. She was ecstatic – until the baby became ill even before birth and then lived only two months in the NICU. Her story shows how we can praise God in the midst of loss and pain.

--Kyla: She'd been a foreign missionary serving God among tribal people for 22 years when she received the shock of her life. Right in front of her eyes, her 19-year old son, a Christian raised on the mission field and soldier in the Army, was arrested for armed robbery of a bank. He was convicted and sent to prison for ten years. Her story reminds us that God could have kept her son from having a part in the robbery, but He allowed it to happen, and we can learn to trust His purposes.

--Judy: Her husband Bobby left for work as maintenance man at a Christian school before she woke that morning. When she kissed him at bedtime the night before, she was unaware she'd never see him alive again. He had a massive heart attack at work and she was suddenly thrust into widowhood. Her story shows the tender hand of God as He prepares the way before us.

--Sharon: She went from being a happy homemaker and fitness instructor to being beset by trial after trial and then becoming a fighter of cancer in various parts of her body. Six years ago, one of her great desires was to see her little one year old granddaughter celebrate one more Christmas. She has now celebrated six Christmases and has five grandchildren. God has given her peace as she undergoes treatment for yet another cancer diagnosis.

--Mary: Her 22-year old son Chas was a handsome, hard-working young man, friendly and loved by all who knew him. He'd just asked his girlfriend to marry him and they had looked at engagement rings that week. Mary's phone rang that morning with the sudden news that Chas was dead, killed instantly when his work truck ran off the road on a foggy curve and crashed into a tree. Her story reminds us how God will be there with us in our darkest hour.

--**Elizabeth**: With two teenagers at home and a thriving career as a teacher and writer, she began losing control of her body and was crushed to hear a diagnosis of MS. Gradually, the disease crept through her muscles until she needed help with even the simplest functions. Still in the prime of life, how do you cope with day to day dependence and an unknown future? How do you redefine your identity?

--**Eleanor:** A single mother struggling to support herself and two young children, asked God to provide them with a home. He answered her prayer and the miracle of that event still bolsters her faith. Her story shows God's hand of mercy as He lovingly provides for His children.

--**Lora**: How do you forgive the man who murdered your mother? When she was only 14 years old, her mother, a Christian school teacher, was brutally shot and killed by a student in a school shooting. Although the pain of her loss still haunts her, she reveals how God changed bitter hatred into full forgiveness.

--**Sandy**: She watched her active, young husband become an invalid after his liver failed and a liver transplant backfired so badly he spent 20 months in ICU before finally succumbing to pneumonia. As she copes with this tragedy, she also cares for two young daughters who have insulin-dependent diabetes – and are heartbroken at the loss of their Daddy. Her constant comfort is the fact that God knew all of this was going to happen and He is in control of it all.

--**Cindy**: When she was born, the doctor said, "We never should have let this baby live." Her childhood was beset by surgeries, struggle and guilt. Even though she was saved in her mid-teens and married a Christian, she was still haunted by guilt and feelings of worthlessness. Continuing health problems added to the toxic mix and divorce was the result. How does God heal gaping spiritual and emotional wounds and bring about restoration?

--**Shannon**: For ten years she and her husband prayed for a baby. They even mortgaged their home to pay for rounds of in vitro and suffered the crushing failure of every effort. Her husband turned to drugs and their marriage was on the verge of collapse when God stepped in and gradually healed every problem. God works in mysterious ways His glory to show.

--**Lynda & Chip:** While Lynda's story is dramatic in itself, Chip's story only makes their situation doubly difficult, so I had to include his amazing story alongside that of Lynda. When Lynda suddenly became ill eight years ago and lost the ability to do almost anything, Chip was beside her, helping all the way, until she improved more than any doctor thought possible. Then, six years later, as he sought to be a Good Samaritan on the interstate highway, a driver lost control and Chip's leg was cut from his body. What happens to Christians when the ax of tragedy falls twice?

GRETCHEN

Gretchen was asked the question, "What do you think of the statement in Alfred Lord Tennyson's poem that reads: "'Tis better to have loved and lost than never to have loved at all?'"

Gretchen answered: "Oh, I definitely agree with those words. I don't regret that it happened. In spite of everything I went through, the experience of loving lil Shawn and having him love me back was worth it."

If anyone is qualified to answer that question, it would be Gretchen. Here is her story:

Gretchen was 44-years old when it happened. She'd been married 13 years and long ago been told she could not have a baby. Although she'd always longed to be a mother, over the years she'd developed peace about her childlessness and accepted her situation as part of God's plan.

As a leader in the children's ministries at her church, she'd become like a second mother to many of her friends' children. One of her joys was having "Princess" retreats for the young girls and encouraging them to grow in the beauty and grace of our Lord.

So -- it was a huge surprise when Gretchen discovered she was pregnant. It was a surprise and joy that a dream she'd given up on was at last coming true! She would be a mother with a precious baby of her very own -- praise God from who all blessings flow!

No sooner had Gretchen shared her exciting news with family and friends than word came from her doctors that the pregnancy was in trouble. The baby boy she was carrying had a condition known as Intrauterine Growth Restriction (IUGR) which meant that abnormalities in the placenta restricted the delivery of oxygen and nutrients to the baby. It was then they told her and her husband Shawn that their son might "pass away at any time."

How do expectant parents cope with such news? Gretchen's life had seemed like a placid stream before she'd been placed on a roller coaster that started off with joyous promise, but was now plunging into a dark and fearful place.

Her first reaction was quite natural -- tears, an overwhelming sorrow and her heart's cry, "Lord, please no! This cannot be happening!!!"

Almost immediately, hope eased the sorrow. She said, "For a while, it was hope that conquered my sadness -- the hope that the Lord would heal my son and that what they'd predicted would be wrong -- that he would be born a miracle....a complete miracle."

Months passed and the roller coaster continued its twisting journey of ups and downs -- sometimes hopeful, but more often news they did not want to hear. It was a frightening ride for Gretchen and Shawn. Early in her pregnancy she was admitted to the hospital and placed on bed rest. This tiny baby boy, whom they'd named Shawn Austin, was a little fighter, and he'd surprised the doctors by refusing to quietly "pass away" as they'd predicted. The expectant mother was full of hope as she wrote, "We are still praying, and not giving up on this miracle baby."

As a friend watching this heart-wrenching situation unfold from a distance, what touched my heart most deeply was Gretchen's firm and unwavering statement: "I still will love and serve Him - no matter what!" This was not just something she said to sound spiritual. Even through tears and sorrow, Gretchen meant what she said from the bottom of her broken heart. That was powerful to me -- and still is as she reaffirms her love for God every day.

On the morning of July 1, 2011, Shawn Austin came into the world with eyes wide open and a strong yet gentle cry. There was joy at his birth and a continued hope that this sick 'lil warrior, as Gretchen calls him, would survive and be a testament to God's miraculous grace.

But, it was not to be. This beautiful baby boy with dark hair and a sweet smile spent the entire 2-1/2 months of his life in the intensive care unit at the Children's Hospital. His Mommy and Daddy loved him and loved on him as much as they possibly could. Gretchen said, "Shawn was a fighter until the end of his precious but brief life when he went home to be with Jesus."

How did Gretchen cope with such loss?

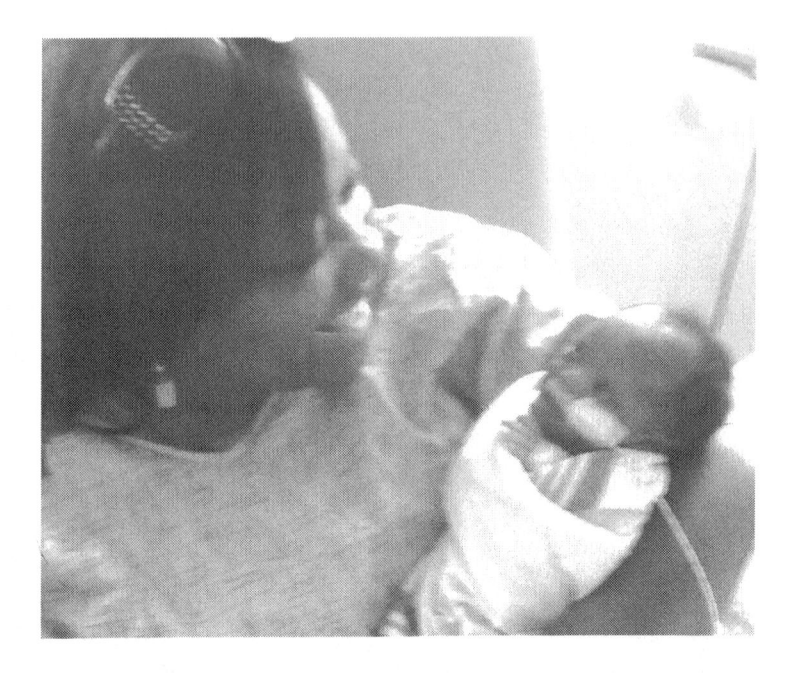

Gretchen and her son in the NICU

When a woman loses her precious baby, it is heart-rending, but it seemed like Gretchen's loss had an extra twist that made it even worse.

During moments of weakness, you can imagine satanic influences whispering in her ear, "What kind of God would dangle the carrot of motherhood in front of you like that? After you'd long ago accepted your childlessness, why would He set you up for a fall by giving you the joy of pregnancy and a glimpse of your baby, only to dash your hopes and joys with pain and a sorrow like you'd never known before? What kind of God does that?"

These are the thoughts and feelings of the natural self -- which is still part of all of us, but such thoughts and feelings are destructive to every part of who we are -- and unfair to every part of who God is.

Gretchen knows this and refused to let Satan bait her into blaming God, or letting bitterness cloud her world.

Gretchen explains, "My peace with God is knowing that His ways are perfect; that He chose me to parent that Lil Warrior and Blessing that he was. There's no recurring bitterness or anger with the Lord. My pain now is to have had a child that was taken back to heaven so quickly, missing him and just what he would have added to our lives; feeling emptiness in my arms though my heart is full of the love that I felt for him. My healing is a work in progress, but He that has begun a good work in me shall complete it to the end!"

Our God of love does not take joy in our sorrow and pain. Did Jesus not cry at the grave of Lazarus because our sorrows touch Him so deeply? "One thing I have learned," Gretchen says, "is that during the most tragic, the most awful and the worst thing that I have endured to date, is that God is still faithful, and that He is still able in whatever He does and in however He does it. I have come to love and trust Him even more."

One of the passages of scripture that has helped comfort Gretchen's heart is found in 2 Corinthians 1:3-4: "*Blessed be the God and Father of our Lord Jesus Christ, the Father of mercies and God of all comfort, who comforts us in all our tribulation, that we may be able to comfort those who are in any trouble, with the comfort with which we ourselves are comforted by God.*"

When Gretchen was saved at the age of nine years old at a Good News Club at her Aunt Joyce's house, it was the love of Jesus that drew her to the Savior. Little did she know what ups and downs of life lay ahead of her. None of us know what the years will bring -- what path the Lord will call us to follow. One thing we *can* count on along the way is that "*He will never leave us nor forsake us*" Hebrews 13:5.

Gretchen knows that everything in God's plan is for a purpose. A few months before lil Shawn was born, she went to see Christian speaker Priscilla Shirer's simulcast, "Life Interrupted," based on her Bible study on the Book of Jonah.

After seeing the simulcast, Gretchen wrote in an email, "I learned that *life interruptions* are God's Divine Appointments whether positive and/or negative. God is not shocked by the interruption. If He didn't cause it, He allowed it. He wants to see how we handle it -- what are we to do with this thing, and will we go to the Nineveh that is usually associated with such an interruption? The interruption becomes invitation to walk in the will of God for our lives. I do believe EVMS (Eastern Virginia Medical School – where she received her medical care during pregnancy) is my Nineveh. Instead of running from the Lord and the Nineveh that He wants us to go to, we need to go and see how He sets us up for a season of power that we have never known and/or experienced before!

"It is one thing to read about it, but it is another to experience God's power in your life and situation. And lastly, one of the things that I learned personally for myself this weekend is this: The decisions that I make today with the opportunity that God gives me will leave marks on the lives of those who come in contact with me. This blessed interruption in my life has a greater purpose than just fulfilling my desire to be a mom! God wants and is doing something great in me, my husband, our marriage and in the lives of those we come in contact with. God doesn't make mistakes and this will be for our good and His glory!!! Our transformation is hinging on our response to the Lord -- our love and obedience...which for me is one and the same!"

Gretchen's response to the Lord has never wavered. Even after the loss of her beloved son, she said, "I prayed and asked the Lord to fill the Shawn-sized hole in my heart with Christ Himself; that He will take the brokenness and transform it into something so glorious that others have no choice but to see and know that it comes from Him; that I look like an extraordinary freak of human nature and though it is known that I hurt and that I hurt deeply, God was so gracious and loving in meeting me there."

Gretchen continued: "In the lyrics of one of the songs that means so much to me right now, I want glory to meet my suffering and that it will bring me back to life even though a part of me has died. I want the Lord to take the part of me (my heart) that died and breathe it back to life. That the hurt, the pain and anguish I have experienced out of this journey will not be in vain. As for my relationship with the Lord, my purpose for being, loving and serving Him, I would like to hear Him say, 'Well done, Gretchen -- even in your grieving. And for whatever purpose that I use it to bless others when the time is right.'"

When I see Gretchen, I see a strong woman with a beautiful, joyful spirit. The love of Christ radiates from her and I can see that her great desire is to please God and bring glory to His name. Her faithfulness and testimony are an inspiration to me – and to all who see her.

What sticks with me most from Gretchen's story is the statement she made even before she knew the outcome of her and lil Shawn's journey. I tear up with emotion every time I think of her heartfelt words, "I still will love and serve Him - no matter what!"

This is the heart of the issue – and Gretchen's heart remains true to her God – no matter what.

Photo: – Courtesy photo of Gretchen and Shawn Austin in the NICU (neo-natal intensive care unit) of the hospital where he was born.

KYLA

Life can turn upside down in the blink of an eye. Kyla knows just how frightening such a turn can be. Here is her story:

It all began on an ordinary day. Kyla and her husband Darryl were adjusting to life back in America while on home assignment from their work in tribal missions on an island in the Pacific. They'd spent over 20 years with their four children, living in a thatch-roofed house on stilts, surrounded by exotic trees and gentle people who'd invited them into their village. These were people who, while they had a name for God, didn't know anything about Him. They were desirous of eternal life, and greatly feared death. When they heard the missionaries wanted to tell them about God and eternal life, they were eager to hear.

Over the years, Darryl and Kyla translated books of the Bible into the native language and taught the people how to read that Word. As soon as the people heard about sin and salvation, heaven and hell, and the wonderful love of God, many accepted the Word as truth. They grew into a Christian village that eventually reached out to others with the Good News.

Kyla and Darryl's faithfulness, and God's power made great inroads for the Kingdom in that place. As so often happens on this sinful earth in which we live, Satan delights in attacking the "cream of the crop" and he goes out of his way to turn the screws on some of the dearest of God's servants.

It all happened so fast –

Kyla had enjoyed a two-mile run that morning with her 20-year old son Chad – a rare pleasure since he was stationed at an Army base 3,000 miles away on the opposite coast. During their run, they'd had a chance to catch up on their last 18 months apart. They were excited about the upcoming week together as a family.

Later on, they were in the front yard chatting with his younger brother and sisters on the porch – enjoying a few moments together before they all headed to church for a family picture for the new church directory.

Suddenly, a car barreled into their short driveway. A door swung open even before the car came to a stop. Two men jumped out and asked Chad his name. When he answered, they ordered him to spread his hands on their car. In the blink of an eye, he was handcuffed and put into a second car.

Kyla was stunned and dazed. She said, "My mind was numb, but I remember thinking, 'My son has done something to get himself in trouble or knows someone else who has. But, to be arrested by the FBI?' Nothing made sense – just didn't compute! How...why...? Thus began our nightmare."

Chad at the age of 1 year

As it turned out, Chad had been involved in a bank robbery near the base where he was stationed on the west coast shortly before he'd come home for a visit. Kyla and Darryl learned the details along with the rest of the nation. When they stepped out of the courthouse after their son's arraignment, reporters thrust microphones at them, asking for their response to the crime. Shock and confusion shone from their faces on the local newscast as they sought to answer questions they still did not understand themselves. They found themselves in a situation they never dreamed they'd ever experience.

Kyla said, "We were stupefied as to how he could have gotten involved in something like this. He had no history of any kind of misbehavior. He was a quiet thinker, though a follower and I guessed his choice of friends had something to do with this situation."

As the reality of what had happened sunk in, Kyla said she experienced a range of emotion: bafflement, hurt, regret and compassion. She said, "I was not angry at Chad, only angry at the thoughtlessness the crime indicated. Did he not think of what this would mean for him, for his family, his close friends, his future?"

Chad was sentenced by the judge to 35 years for his crime, which ended up being an 11 year sentence in prison.

Ten years have passed since the beginning of this tragic episode in their lives. Here are Kyla's answers to questions about her experience:

Q. What have you learned from your tragedy that you might share with other sisters?
A. "When we submit to God, we heal more quickly." She then added, "I realized that we do our best before God to raise and train our children in the way they should go, but in the end, they make their own choices. I think it also taught us more empathy and understanding for people in crisis. And also, I learned that people in prison are normal people who have simply made wrong choices or maybe been wrongfully accused. They have the same basic needs as anyone else."

Q. Have you grown in your walk with God?
A. "I've experienced the solidifying of God's truth in my heart and life. Seeing passages of scripture that I had studied previously come to guide my thoughts and keep me on an even keel has been thrilling."

Q. Are you still healing, ten years later?
A. "The loss will always be painful, but always soothed by God's comfort of scriptures, like, *'Be still and know that I am God'* and *'Casting all your care upon Him, for He cares for you.'* We can let these things devour and destroy us, or we can trust our God who has proven Himself faithful and caring over and over again."

Q. What were some things that helped you?
A. "It has been amazing to experience the love and care of the body of Christ. Besides God's Word, the thing that kept me going and helped me get up in the morning was the many emails that people sent, sharing verses, prayers and just encouragement – it was huge! My sister and her husband gave up their planned weeks' vacation to be with us in the early days – what pillars of strength they were! Many came to share in our pain and pray for us.

Also, something Dr. David Jeremiah wrote in Turning Point that says, *'We can't always control what happens to us, but we are responsible for our response. It takes time to work through painful and injurious episodes in life; but nothing is wasted in the providence of God. He knows how to take every burden and bring from it a blessing. Obstacles are stepping stones, not roadblocks.'*"

Q. What scripture helped you most?
A. "There are so many, but the passage that God used to help me most in the first days was, *'Love the Lord with all your heart, soul and mind'* and *'Whatsoever things are true...'*

Through Elisabeth George's wonderful book *Loving God With Your Mind*, I had been learning what it means to love God with my mind, so in those early days, I knew that dwelling in the past (like what did we do wrong? what should we have done differently? I failed as a parent! etc.) was not loving God with my mind. Thinking to the future (like: how many years will he get? Will he be harmed in prison? Will my husband and I see him in freedom again? ... especially Darryl since he found out he had diabetes not long after our son's arrest) was not loving God with my mind. So, focusing on what is true right now helped me to love and trust God for today by putting one step in front of the other -- doing what He wanted me to do today.

Another verse I dwelt onto was in Jeremiah 29:11, *"'I know the plans I have for you,' declares the Lord, 'plans to prosper you and not to harm you, plans to give you hope and a future.'"* I cling to that promise for ourselves and for our son."

Q. What has been one of the hardest adjustments?
A. "That life doesn't stop. We had to go on living – sort of without him. We grieved as though he were lost to us, but we had to adjust to a new

norm. We have three other children that needed our attention. To have so many family pictures, but he is not in them...to have memories that he is not sharing...having his sisters and brother get married and he not being there – that is sad."

Q. Did you ever say to God, "This is just not fair?"
A. "Can the clay say to the potter, what are you doing? As our Creator, He has total right to do anything with us that He deems best. God knows what He is doing and He is always good. He could have done a myriad of things to change the situation so that our son did not put himself in that position. But God allowed him to go down that path and I can only thank Him that if he was heading to a life of destruction, that He stopped him in his tracks. I trust God to work in his life and use him for His glory."

One morning on my walk, as I passed over the bridge, water gushed from a fountain in the lake, so beautiful reflecting in the early morning sunlight. A familiar song came to my mind:

> 'I've got a river of life flowing out of me,
> Makes the lame to walk and the blind to see,
> Opens prison doors, sets those captives free.
> Spring up oh well, and give to me
> That life abundantly.'

Then I thought of my son in prison surrounded by so many who don't know Jesus. Our son is a child of God and therefore has a river of life flowing out of him. I began to pray that he would be a channel of blessing to others; that the river of life flowing out of him would draw them to the great Life-giver and that the prison doors of their souls would be opened and they would be free indeed, able to experience abundant life. Hearing of times he impacted other lives gave eternal value to his incarceration."

Q. When were you saved?
A. I was saved two days before my sixth birthday. My mother was teaching us about the Israelites crossing of the Red Sea and their deliverance from Egyptian bondage. She explained the need for our deliverance from God's wrath and the power, penalty and bondage of sin.

Not long after my son's arrest, I was studying in Exodus and reading again the story of Moses and his family. I was struck with the similarities that the stories of Jochabed and Moses had with Chad and I. Both our sons had an unusual upbringing (Moses under Egyptian tutelage, our son homeschooling and on the mission field, with High School at a boarding school); they both committed a crime seemingly out of the blue and they both were 'sent away' for a number of years. Moses ended up with a huge responsibility given to him by God and became 'the friend of God.' Who knows what God will do for Chad? We do know he has had impact on others during his time behind the barbed wire.

We never read whether Jochabed saw Moses alive again after he grew up. I'm sure she suffered anguish and questioned God, perhaps saying, 'I went to great lengths to save Moses as a baby, gave him over to Pharaoh's daughter, and then, it comes to this?'

I too, felt much of what Jochabed must have felt… so many questions.

Jochabed has become my hero and will be one of the first people I look for in heaven!"

Q. What advice would you share with other sisters?
A. "When we have difficulty in our relationships or with events in our lives, remember that God is not our enemy, and our relatives/friends are not our enemy. The enemy of our souls is Satan and he will do anything to defeat you, to make you turn away from God or at least become ineffective as a witness for God. If we are going to be angry, be angry at Satan and the way he has messed things up. God loves us deeply and only allows in our lives what He knows to be for our ultimate good and His glory. Lean into Him!!!"

As we end our visit with Kyla, she shares a recent precious time she had with the Lord:

"I love to walk in the cool and quiet of the early morning. I have many talks with God during those times. My route often passes through a neighborhood park. The park boasts a small lake with a bridge arching over the water. Seagulls often line up on either side of the railing. They scatter as soon as I approach, fly around over my head and, as I walk off the bridge, they land back on the rail behind me. I love watching their behavior and even find myself talking to them.

One morning as I approached the bridge, I noticed immediately that there were no birds…anywhere! That seemed strange. I said out loud, 'Awww! No birds today? Where are you? You mean you will not be here to comfort me? I looked forward to seeing you.'

By this time I was midway across the empty bridge. Then, from the direction of the river, I saw a V of birds flying toward me. I stopped and watched as they passed behind me, went around the middle of the lake and circled around in front of me again before flying off toward the river. I smiled. I knew God had sent them just for me and I sensed His loving arms around me, holding me close in His tender embrace. Thank you, Father."

"He that dwelleth in the secret place of the most High
Shall abide under the shadow of the Almighty.
I will say of the Lord, He is my refuge and my fortress.
My God, in Him will I trust" Psalm 91:1-2

~NOTE: Chad was released from prison two months before the completion of this book and he has returned to his family. Kyla said, "It is because of God's grace to Chad and our family and through the prayers of so many around the world, that Chad has returned to us healthy in mind, body and soul. We are eternally grateful to all who had a part in that! May God be glorified!"

Photos: - Courtesy photo of Chad as a child on the mission field.
 -- The two seagulls are of foreign descent since I saw them on a walkway in Zurich, Switzerland. They're standing in for Kyla's local birds. SJB

JUDY

~Judy Shares her Story:

"March, 2007 - I remember it well. On Sunday, March 11, my husband Bobby took our grandson Josh to church while I stayed home recuperating from an intestinal virus. After church, Bobby came home and we had lunch together – he ate a sub while I ate a bowl of Jello, but that was OK, because Bobby had come home to be with me instead of going out to eat with Josh as we usually did after church.

That afternoon, we spent more time doing things together than we normally did. We enjoyed swinging on our front porch swing, talking and relaxing together.

We lived in a rural area so we strolled around our yard and the edge of the woods behind our house. We were big into gardening, so we looked for the jonquils blooming, yellow flowers on the forsythia bush, clematis buds and periwinkle blooms peeking up along the edge of our yard, enjoying early signs of spring. With feeders and plenty of seeds in our yard, there are always birds singing that time of day and they serenaded us on our walk. We had a very pleasant and special afternoon and night together. Except for missing church, it had been a beautiful day.

Since God knows the future, He'd planned that wonderful day my husband and I spent together. God knew the assurance that our last time together was full of happy memories would help me be able to endure the rest of that week and would bring comfort to me for the rest of my life.

Thank you Lord for the pleasant memory of our last day together.

Monday morning around 10am, I received a phone call from the office of our church-school. Bobby had been working as maintenance man at the Christian school for about nine years (and volunteered for years before that), since retiring from his job with the government. The school secretary told me to get to the hospital as soon as possible because an ambulance was at the school. They had an issue with Bobby.

God only knows how I got dressed and actually drove the 14 miles it took to get to the school. Only He could have gotten me safely to my destination. I'm normally a driver who obeys the speed limit, but that day, I found myself going 20 miles over the speed limit twice. I was so distraught I was almost yelling at a friend who called to see if she could help. Someone had called her to get my cell-phone number, but neither she nor I knew what had happened.

As I neared the school, I called and asked if I should stop by there or continue driving on to the hospital. I was told to stop at the school. When I arrived, the associate pastor, his wife and a very good friend of mine were waiting for me in the parking lot. As soon as I got out of the car, one of them said, "You're going to be alright."

Right then, I knew Bobby had gone to be with the Lord. I was in a state of shock, unable to think clearly, not wanting to believe what I was hearing. He had never mentioned any trouble with his heart (later I found out the doctor was also in a state of shock because she had not detected anything that would cause a heart attack). I was led into a room and sat down with several friends, but I was having trouble answering questions asked by the police. I couldn't think straight.

We were also having trouble getting in touch with my sons and this upset me. I thought -- my sons - how are they going to take the fact that their father just died? One of my sons talked with his father every day and they often did projects together and hunted together. We all fished together. All that would change.

How am I going to keep going? I wondered. *How are we going to make it without his presence on a daily basis?* I was married at the age of 18. I'd never been on my own. Bobby hadn't even been away from me more than a few days our entire married life.

I sat there in a daze. Only through the help of friends and the grace of God did I make it through that morning. I sent two men from our church to go get my dad. When he arrived, he was crying. My dad -- the rock of our family, was almost as upset as I was.

The sudden death of a loved one is an incredible shock – and there are few things more sudden than a massive heart attack. Minutes before his death, Bobby had been laughing with fellow employees, going about his day as usual. He walked away from them, turned the corner going toward one of the houses the school owned when he simply took his final breath and fell to the ground. At least I am comforted by the assurance that he was safe in heaven long before anyone even knew he was gone. The school where Bobby worked had over 800 students (ages 4-18 years). Only God could have arranged it so that none of the students saw him lying on the ground. Most all the students knew him and they all loved Mr. M. *Thank you for a mate that was loved and made others feel good.*

Someone later said, "You didn't even have time to say anything to Bobby." I said that I had 44 years of marriage with him and if I hadn't said it by then, shame on me. But God knew that if I had known what lay ahead on that day, all I would have done was cry. Instead, I have pleasant memories of a day spent together with love and caring. *Thank you Lord that I didn't have to see him suffer.*

The next few days were a blur. Part of the time I was numb and part of the time I wept. Sometimes, I'd simply be walking in a daze. Still, I was able to laugh at times – just as Bobby liked for me to do. He didn't like to see me cry. Only through the help of God was I able to get through those days.

I found it was easier and felt safer for me to stay at my dad's house. Although there were many memories of Bobby there, it wasn't like going home – a place with memories that surrounded me and threatened to suffocate me with reminders of what I'd just lost.

My sister took my dad and cared for him while people piled into his house. I went through the motions of pretending I had everything under control. Even though when I'd been a church secretary I'd helped many people cope when there'd been a death in their family, I forgot several things I wanted done that I should have remembered. I just wasn't all there, even though I pretended that I was.

Friends and family stepped in with support and physically helped me get through those difficult days. I stayed with my dad (89 years old) for the first few days. My teenage granddaughter stayed with me the first night I actually spent in my house without Bobby. God gave me that amazing *"peace of God that passes all understanding"* Philippians 4:7, and after the first night I was on my own -- just me and God. The outpouring of love and support at the funeral home visitation, funeral (overflow of people at both), and at my home was amazing. *Thank you Lord, for such support and love.*

Here's another example of God preparing the way before us: the younger of my two sons has lived most of his adult life in other countries with his job, but during the spring of 2007, he was living here – only a few miles away. He and his wife and young daughter had been able to spend time with Bobby during those months before his passing – important to them all. And – they were here for me when I needed them most. *Again I thanked God for my son and his family being here.*

My oldest son had a little talk with my dog Sugar. He told her that the two of them would now have to take care of me. Sugar was not accustomed to staying inside the house very long, but she laid on the floor by my side each night for weeks. When I moved to another room of the house, she followed me. It was almost uncanny how she seemed to sense my need for her company during that time of adjustment.

My son and his family lived just down the street from us at that time. They graciously stepped in and took care of projects that had been left undone by his father. *Thank you Lord, for my constant care.*

I never stopped attending church after Bobby died. My church is like family and I needed them. I did change Sunday School classes, because not seeing Bobby sitting in his regular seat in the couples class hurt too much. My grandson Josh, who went to church with me, always accompanied his granddad and I out to lunch after church. We discovered that we needed to pick different places to eat lunch after church, because it was just not the same. *I thank the Lord for the time spent with my grandson.*

I continued to work with young children on Wednesday night at our church, served on a couple of committees and did special things for others (all things that I still do). Bible studies, Sunday School, church services, conversations with other Christians and reading about others in similar situations have continued to be an up-lift of my faith and spirit. *Thank you Lord for helping me to stay strong in my faith to you.*

The week after the funeral, the after-school day-care children sent me cards they had made as a tribute to Bobby and as an encouragement to me. These young children made flowers out of crepe paper, drew pictures and wrote notes such as, "We love Mr. M," and "we miss Mr. M," and "we are praying for you." I still have each of these precious notes.

A short time later, the older students and teachers wrote things about how much he'd meant to them and one of the teachers put them into a book for me. Many of the notes talked about his kind smile (which I also loved), his helpfulness and his friendly ways. Some spoke of his abilities to build things, fix things and his willingness to help out in time of need (and there is a constant need at a private school). At the end of the book was a big sign "WELL DONE - GOOD AND FAITHFUL SERVANT."

Thank you Lord, again you are showing me how much you and others care.

Since we were living off of my husband's retirement from his previous job and part of his employment from the school, I was a little unsure about my financial status with him gone. Again, as our Sunday School class puts it, *"God is good all the time. All the time God is good."*

A friend offered me a part-time job at her place of business. This gave me a steady income and time to take care of my business, my aging father, and my home with ten acres of land that needed caring for. Not only did the job help out until I could get my finances straight, my employer was a big source of comfort and a dear friend when I needed it most.

The Lord has not only provided financially for me, but given me a little extra that I might be able to help others as well. I continue to serve the Lord with my tithes and offerings and have never missed a meal for lack of food. *Thank you Lord for answering my need.*

For years before Bobby's death, I had a severe back problem. Thankfully, I had surgery that corrected the problem while Bobby was alive and could help me recuperate. I'm further thankful, because the correction of that back problem made it possible for me to take care of many things that I would have been unable to do before surgery – things I used to rely on Bobby to do. *I again thank God for taking care of me in advance of my urgent need and making it possible for me to care for myself.*

I felt too young to be cast into the role of widow. Sixty-two might not sound young to others, but I'd anticipated at least another twenty or thirty years together. Now, I was no longer a *wife*, a title I'd enjoyed wearing for 44 years. Now, my remaining years would be spent as *widow*. I had never lived alone, never been without Bobby for more than a few days. I'm a people-person and really didn't want to face living for twenty-plus years all alone. *Lord, this is going to be so hard. You are really going to have to get me through this.*

At first I really didn't know who I was or what I wanted to do. I had been a child under my parents trying to please them; then a wife trying to please my husband; then a mother trying my best to take care of my two little boys. Through the years, I felt that the Lord should come first, but I also felt the importance of being an obedient child, loving wife, and caring mother. Now, these roles were no longer mine – I felt lost. I cried out to God, "*Who am I, Lord and what do you want me to do with the rest of my life?*"

All the *firsts* are very hard -- birthdays without your spouse, anniversaries, Thanksgiving, Christmas, Valentine's Day and anything that is special -- like grandchildren getting married, babies being born. It all becomes times of mixed emotions – happy occasions, but mixed with sadness that Bobby is not here to share them with us. I now have three great-grandchildren that I know Bobby would have loved and adored. I'm so happy to have these precious little additions to the family, yet I feel incredibly sad that he is not here to see them – and that they will never know him either. *Thank you Lord for enlarging our family.*

The Lord never promised there would be no tears. But in Hebrews 13:5, He did promise, *"I will never leave thee nor forsake thee."* The Lord gave me the ability to laugh easily, but that ability also comes with the other side of the coin -- tearing up easily. I admit to having cried a bucket full of tears since I lost Bobby. At first it didn't take much for the tears to flow -- a simple problem, something special I would see and want to share with him, someone mentioning something he did or said could have the tears running down my face and all the way into my lap. Now after years without him, the waterworks can still start when I need him with me through health problems, or try to get something done that he would have had no problem with, or just when the loneliness of not having him around hits me.

Even through the tears, I have relied on the verse in Hebrews many, many times -- it always comforts me. Over and over again through the eight years I've spent alone since Bobby's sudden passing, God has proven to be a comfort and source of strength. I have friends who pray for me and go off with me and help in times of need, but God is the one who is with me through every minute of every day. This is the promise that gets me through the good times and the bad times and helps me sleep at night. *Thank you Lord for never leaving me nor forsaking me!*

And then, there's that final memory that God tenderly prepared for me. Knowing it was our last night together, God gave us the loving closeness of falling to sleep with our arms wrapped around each other. Since I'd been sick, Bobby didn't wake me when he left that morning and so I was unable to say good-bye to him. My last memory of my husband is his kind, gentle closeness as I fell asleep.

Thank you Lord for blessing me with that final, sweet memory that you knew I would need."

Photo: The pretty daffodils representing Judy's flowers, were in a pot at the entrance of the Baseball Hall of Fame in Cooperstown, New York. It was a beautiful sunny day in spring. SJB

-Courtesy photo of Judy and Bobby on their wedding day.

SHARON

I was introduced to Sharon's story by my sister Ava, who knows this lovely woman from a church she attended while living in another state. After telling me a bit about Sharon's struggles, Ava showed me a piece Sharon had written for their church's annual Advent Devotional Book in 2014. Here is an excerpt:

"We say, "I hope" a lot, especially around the holidays. I hope all the family can get together this year. I hope I don't overcook the turkey. I hope I can get everything done on my 'To Do' list. I hope I get that special gift I have been hinting about. What we really mean is, "I wish." 'I wish' is based on our desires, the ingenuity of ourselves or others motivated towards pleasing us.

Hebrews 11:1 teaches us that real hope is brought about by faith, and FAITH is only as potent as the object of our faith. 'Now faith is the assurance of things hoped for, the conviction of things not seen.' Being certain of God is the hope that sustains us in all times.

Five Christmases ago, I was facing the first of my major cancer surgeries and, quite frankly, hoping to make it until the next Christmas season. I hoped to watch my little granddaughter, aged 1 ½ years, open gifts and hear the Baby Jesus story again and again. I was hoping in the ONE who can provide hope.

I am still asking God for more Christmases, and I am so very thankful that I am approaching this advent season with FIVE beautiful grandchildren. I am thankful for the God of whom Isaiah spoke: "From ages past no one has heard, no ear has perceived, no eye has seen any God besides you, who works for those who wait for him." (Isaiah 64:4)."

Sharon & Brent with their five grandchildren

-Sharon Shares her Story:

"For a while, I felt my life was charmed. I had a handsome, godly husband and three bright, beautiful children, a nice home and a strong network of friends and family. God had smiled on me -- and I liked it.

Although I did not necessarily feel like a "shoe would inevitably drop," there were moments of uncertainty, especially when folks started getting laid off from their jobs at the chemical plant where my husband was employed as an engineer. I remember saying to God in my prayers, "You KNOW I couldn't handle THAT, Lord!"

I can laugh now at how ludicrous that must have sounded to my Creator who well knew the many trials, tests, and struggles He would not only help me to handle, but cause His glory to be revealed through in the years ahead.

Yes, my husband was laid off from his job, along with 200 other management level employees one dark day. As a stay-at-home mother of three young children, I was bewildered and shaken. The job market was flooded with qualified engineers. It was a protracted time of leanness and trust building. There were many humbling ways God provided when we did not know how He would.

It had been 18 months of trusting and trying. I could see that my husband was at his lowest point emotionally. I urged him to go workout at the gym one morning. He happened to meet a man at the gym – a man who offered him a temporary job, which led to another job and finally a permanent job opportunity opened in Georgia.

This was another huge smile of God for me because it was an area where we had vacationed with extended family for several years. It was a beautiful seaside island with a strong Christian community. I called it *Mayberry-by-the-Sea*. Whew!! That was surely the shoe that had dropped. We'd weathered the storm and now it was time to coast!

As we know, there is no such thing as coasting in the Christian life. You are either climbing, or sliding, and the trials are usually the times that I have found that God has led me to gain the most spiritual ground.

There came a season, amidst the joy of raising three teenagers towards young adulthood, when the climb became a bit steeper. My husband's father died suddenly of heart failure, my father died of prolonged heart disease, and my mother fell ill to ovarian cancer and dementia. After the funerals of two of these three loved ones, I was wiped out emotionally and unprepared for the question my husband would pose to me over coffee one summer evening. He asked me, 'If I need a criminal lawyer, who do you think we should call?'

You can only imagine the many adjectives that could describe my stunned response. My husband is and has always been -- a Christian man of integrity and a proverbial 'straight arrow.' How could he possibly be in a position to need a criminal lawyer?

Suddenly – and through no fault of his own -- he was facing federal indictment for his role in management of a chemical plant charged with multiple environmental violations. The details of this trial could fill a book, but the bottom line is that after two years and a very expensive legal battle, Brent had to serve an 18 months sentence in a low security federal prison.

This time I asked, "God, can YOU handle this with me -- FOR me?" He did -- and with amazing grace and glory for Himself.

The Christian community where we lived, along with family and friends from all over, helped in every way imaginable. Money was raised to help me with everything from house payments to groceries. Cards were mailed to him to open every day he was incarcerated. He was reelected a deacon in our church even though he was absent. His present employers held his job and even sent him work to do. He was able to attend Bible study several times a week within the walls of confinement, making new friends and encouraging other Christian men along the way. Our church even paid for the Beth Moore study of the Life of David for him to lead while he was there. I was able to send their thank you notes directly to Beth.

I visited Brent every weekend, but still led the Singles Sunday School class. We were committed. One of the class members changed the oil in my car and another one colored my hair for free. Heaven knows there were quite a few gray ones popping out!

Even today, 15 years after this time, my husband is totally committed to Kairos Prison Ministry, visiting residents with the love of God – and special thanks for God's mercy for him and for us as a family.

About the time Brent was to be released to a half-way house and be able to return to work, I discovered that our son had become involved with taking drugs and was acting out in anger and rebellion. My mother died during this stressful season, as well.

I had never known such pain. I felt the enemy was within the walls. Before, I felt the attack had been to the walls of our 'family fortress' – now, it had taken a more personal turn. God was teaching me to trust -- and He still is today. No more details are needed about that situation. I don't like to remember many of the episodes we endured during that season, but rather want to celebrate the progress made to date. God is redeeming it and is faithful to Himself and His purposes.

As for me, I've always loved fitness and the wonder of the workings of the human body, so it was a great fit when, after a short career teaching in the public education field, I became a fitness professional. For twenty five years I taught group fitness classes and became a personal trainer. I tried to inspire my clients to be confident and stretch beyond their comfort zone to accomplish their fitness goals. At the age of 56, I began to realize that I too needed to stretch myself. I had become good at what I enjoyed doing, but needed the nudge to branch out with a fitness challenge outside my own comfort zone.

At that time, I had a very athletic client that "hated" running, so we decided to try and get past our negativity towards running by training for a race. We allowed extra time to build up stamina and ended up completing a half marathon together in January of 2008. We were pleased with our accomplishments and also that we'd grown close through the process of stretching our limits. My mantras were often Bible verses that gave me strength and power for the task. A few of my favorites were:

"*I can do all things through Christ who strengthens me*" Philippians 4:13
"*...Run with endurance the race marked out for you*" Hebrews 12:1
"*I press on toward the goal for the prize...*" Philippians 3:14

    The final week before the race, I wrote in my training journal that I noticed an unusual pain under my left breast and through to my back as I ran. Dismissing the feeling as an overtraining phenomenon, I pressed on. The pain, however, persisted and intensified over the next few months, making it almost impossible to do my job of teaching fitness classes. I tried doctor after doctor. All of them were puzzled with my symptoms and tried a variety of treatments including pills, shots, and pictures. Not until I went to a cardiologist to rule out a heart problem was it discovered that I had a liter of fluid in my left chest. At last, I knew what was causing the pain.

    The discovery led to more scans and tests and then surgery to drain the fluid along with a biopsy of tissue for pathology. Results were inconclusive. Another year went by with persistent pain, coughing, and treatments from various doctors. Finally, with an additional surgery and biopsy, in September of 2009, an undisputed diagnosis of cancer was given. The surgeon spoke to me as I lay on the gurney in the recovery room. I was barely coherent as he asked me, "Sharon, do you understand what I just said? You have cancer. I am sorry."

    I heard what he said, but how do you process such life-changing news – alone, in a sterile room? My first thought was one of sympathy for my husband who was about to hear the same news -- alone, in a separate room. Surely that could have been handled a bit better. Nevertheless, it was the truth and the reality of it was sinking in. During this time, I felt a surreal peace surround me, because I knew that God foreknew this diagnosis, could handle it, and had equipped me through many other trails for this very moment.

    It has been 6-1/2 years since the diagnosis of ovarian cancer, stage IV. I have endured two major surgeries since then and quite a few minor ones (what is minor surgery, anyway, if they put you under?).

Through God's grace and the care of excellent doctors, I am still alive and feeling well.

Just this past year, there was another diagnosis -- a dual and deadly cancer called mesothelioma that has been discovered. Despite that news, and all the grueling chemo treatments (over 53 cycles so far), five weeks of radiation, complete hair loss two times, and changes in my physical strength and stamina, I consider my life blessed and bountiful. I sing in the choir, help lead a women's Bible study, and babysit for my grandkids.

Delightfully, I have found that God has been able to use me to help encourage and counsel others diagnosed with cancer in my church and community. It helps to have a comrade in arms when you go to buy your wig! All five of my grandchildren have been born since my first diagnosis, and I do not take lightly the gift of time God has given me to be with them.

My medical team is amazed at how well I have soldiered through the ravages of these two cancers and I'm, even now, enjoying a period of remission. I always thank them, but make sure they hear my testimony that God is doing a great work of healing in me.

I have no idea when I will leave this earth. I am in no hurry. I probably think about that more than the average person, but I'm not afraid. Actually, I feel expectant about the 'move.' Sometimes fear creeps in over just how much pain I will be called on to endure before then, but I look back on how my Lord has led me through every struggle thus far -- peeling back layers of unexpected blessings and wisdom and showing His ultimate control and sufficiency in all things. He pulls me up another steep incline to show me the view He wants me to see in His perfect plan. There are bruises and a bit of breathlessness as we climb together, but I am tethered to Him and have learned to trust my guide – no matter what."

--Written by Sharon Hanson, who adds, "My story is still unfolding"

Photo: Courtesy photo of Sharon, husband Brent, and the five precious grandchildren God has blessed her with to date.

MARY

There's an old song by the Carpenters that says, "Rainy days and Mondays always get me down." Mary has no problem with rainy days - which can turn into wonderful excuses to spend a quiet, cozy day at home. Nor do Mondays and the start of a brand new week full of opportunities get her down.

Mary is one of those upbeat people who faces life with a smile on her face and a song in her heart. But, there is one kind of day that always gets her down – a day that begins with fog. There are occasional mornings when Mary gets up and sees wisps of fog clinging to the trees in her backyard, blotting out the surrounding area in a misty blanket of white. Those are the mornings she wants to crawl back into bed and pull the covers over her head.

Such days are painful reminders of a morning 27 years ago when a fog enshrouded curve in the road claimed the life of her beloved young son, Chas. Mary says, "I hate fog because I feel like it killed my son."

One Monday evening in late September 1988, Chas stopped by his parent's house after work so that his Mom could hem a pair of pants for him. The 22-year old had recently purchased a townhouse; he had a good job, and he'd fallen in love with a beautiful, sweet girl, Amy. In fact, when they left his parent's home that night, the two young lovebirds went out to look at diamond rings.

The day before, Chas had been with the family for Sunday dinner, and spent the afternoon watching ball games on television with his Dad and two younger brothers, Ryan, 15, and Jon, 8.

Mary remembers Chas standing on a chair in her dining room so that she could pin up the hem of his pants. She said, "When he was leaving, we hugged, and the last words we spoke were, 'I love you, Mom,' and 'I love you, Chas.'"

Photo taken in 1983, Chas was 17 years old, with brothers Ryan, age 10, and Jon, age 3

Less than 48-hours later, on Wednesday morning, Mary received the news that her handsome, loving, happy son with his whole life ahead of him, was dead – killed when his work truck slammed into a tree in the thick fog. How does a mother process such heart-rending, unfathomable words?

Mary said her first reaction was to cry out, "No! It's not true," as she nearly collapsed into the arms of her long-time pastor who'd come to her house to deliver the tragic news. "I couldn't believe he was dead. I thought, this has to be a mistake. I had been worried that morning about my two younger sons as they went off to school in the fog – and here, my other son was already dead."

Mary's husband Charles (who was equally distraught) hurried home from work and they were quickly driven to the hospital to identify Chas' body. When they walked into the medical room where Chas lay, she said, "He looked so natural laying there with bits of grass still clinging to his arms. I thought, this is not real."

Their son Ryan, who'd insisted on going with them to see his brother, fell to the floor and was helped up by his dad." I nearly collapsed too, Mary said, "But then, I felt the peace of God come over me like a shield. I am still amazed at that."

Mary had been saved as a young adult, and Charles had given his heart to the Lord as a child. They were very active in their church, teaching and serving in various ways. Their boys had grown up in church, attended Christian school, and been saved at a young age. Theirs had always been a stable, loving home. Yet, one of Mary's first thoughts was that in some way this was her fault. "Like I hadn't been a good enough parent," she said. "I blamed myself, but then I knew that was wrong. I knew God wasn't punishing us. Then, I got mad at myself for not calling Chas on Tuesday night. I had some mixed up thoughts, but then, somehow, God took hold of me and helped me become peaceful. That's what helped me not get angry – God showed me who He was. I was overcome with it. I'd never thought I could live through such a thing, but God got me through it. He even helped me to start comforting other people during this loss."

Even with God's help, it was still hard. Mary said, "Chas and Charles were so close. I think I cried as much for Charles' loss as for mine.

Charles adds a note, saying, "Chas was a gift from God - a blessing and a joy to us all the days of his short life that we shared until his accidental death."

"Death is so final," Mary said, "And I never knew it until I saw my son lying in a casket. You just try to keep breathing and put one foot in front of the other."

Mary said, "I know God does everything for a purpose – and He will not leave us in our grief and give us more than we can bear. It was a comfort to me when my uncle called me six months later to let me know that he had been saved, and put his life in order because of Chas' death. Lots of young guys who knew Chas began to change their lives and start living for the Lord too."

"How do you live with a broken heart the remainder of our life?" Mary asks. "It takes a long time to heal, but you have to want to live for your mate and your other children, but most of all to serve the Lord, even when your heart is so broken you can't even imagine continuing to live."

Over the years, as Mary and her family have continued healing, she said, "It has surprised me that I could be happy and love life again. It's been hard on birthdays and holidays, and seeing all his friends with their families, and thinking how much his younger brothers needed him. It has made our family different, but I'm enjoying life. I've had to learn to trust God's Word – not just know it. We'll always be healing, but in a good way."

One of Mary's favorite scripture passages is Psalm 23, where she is assured that, *"The Lord is my shepherd, I shall not want...Yea, though I walk through the valley of the shadow of death, I will fear no evil; for You are with me; Your rod and Your staff, they comfort me...My cup runs over..."* Mary said, "It has helped me to know that God walks through the valley with me and holds my hand."

If you ask Mary what advice she would share with other sisters, she immediately says, "We need to be at peace with our family. The last time I saw Chas, I gave him a hug and told him I loved him. A day and a half later, he was gone and I would never have a chance to say another word to him. Always part with the best feelings you can for all people you come in contact with, because you may never get to say I'm sorry. We need to keep our lives in order.

Another point Mary wished to share, "Never mind telling someone that you think of the child they lost. Never hesitate to talk about them and even cry for them. It means so much to you. It means the world to me when people do that. You want to know they are not forgotten.

Mary shared one of the humorous stories she likes to remember about Chas, saying, "Chas knew I loved using coupons. One day I went with him to the doctor to get his back checked and afterward, we went to Wendy's for lunch. When we got there, he looked at me with a serious expression, and said, 'Oh, Mom! We can't eat here. I was surprised, and asked, 'Why?'

With a twinkle in his eye, he answered, 'We don't have a coupon.'" Mary laughs at the memory, "He was always so fun!"

With a smile on her face and a tear in her eye, Mary says, "I'm not grieving all the time, but I don't want to ever get over Chas. He was a joy and I'll always miss him.

-Photo: Courtesy picture of Chas and his younger brothers taken five years before he went up to heaven.

MAMA'S STORY

"When the enemy comes in like a flood, the Spirit of the Lord will lift up a standard against him" Isaiah 59:19

We can all expect to encounter floods on the journey of life, but how in the world can you expect to find indwelling joy and peace a Christian is supposed to have in the midst of that flood??

Do you often feel like your life is being flooded with problems? Sometimes it seems that life hands out one blow after another. One problem doesn't get resolved before another problem is nipping at its heels. Sometimes we just feel like we're drowning.

~My Mother's Final Chapter

When my dear mother, Eleanor, was exactly 91 and-a-half years old, she fell while walking in her backyard and broke a hip.

When she got out of bed that morning, she had no idea her life was going to change and never ever be the same again. In fact, she drove to my house earlier that morning in July, and brought me a few tomatoes from her garden. She visited briefly before returning home to finish watering her plants, and enjoy wandering among the flowers and fruit trees and vegetables she loved to cultivate in her yard.

She fell around midday, losing her balance on an uneven bit of ground surrounding one of her particularly beautiful flowering plants. She tried her best to move, but was surprised to find she was unable to move herself even an inch. Thankfully, we'd talked her into getting a security necklace two months earlier, and with a push of the button, help was on the way.

I arrived at the same time as the fire truck and rescue vehicle. I told the medics that I thought it was all surely a mistake -- a false alarm. She'd probably pushed the button by mistake, and she would be embarrassed that we had all showed up. I mean -- my mother always seemed so strong and indestructible to me.

Sadly, there was no mistake. She wasn't indestructible after all and a shattered hip would prove to be her nemesis. Her life was never the same – not for a single one of the 876 days she continued living on this earth.

She felt as if a flood had crushed life as she knew it. Each day was a struggle for her. How could she be expected to have joy in the final stages of her journey when she could barely navigate her walker and her failing memory was a constant worry to her?

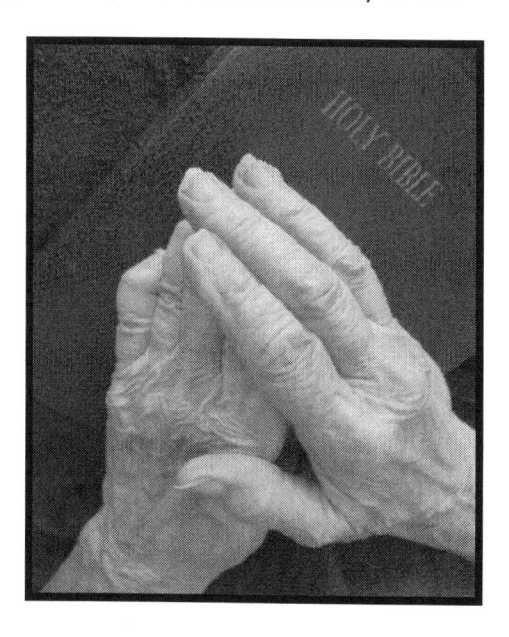

In spite of the sorrow that had befallen her, God's precious love and tenderness was still there, working behind the scenes in the beautiful promise shown in Isaiah where He says our bodies have been, *"upheld by Me from birth...even to your old age, I am He, and even to gray hairs I will carry you!"* 46:3-4.

Flood waters can be devastating. They can ruin homes and vehicles and cause loss of life. Flood waters can also be beneficial -- as in the annual flooding of the Nile River and its spread of rich soil into nearby fields and deserts, resulting in miles of lush green and colorful flowers.

Even though my own life has only been mildly dampened by problems, difficulties flooding the lives of family and friends (and don't forget the swirl of pandemonium flooding the entire world) have splashed over me to such an extent I'm sometimes gasping for breath and looking around for a boat to lift me from the rising tide as well. How can we cultivate an attitude of peace and joy when we're surrounded by waves of suffering?

In her book, *Jesus Calling*, Sarah Young writes as if God is speaking to us, saying: "Though many things feel random and wrong, remember that I am sovereign over everything. I can fit everything into a pattern for good, but only to the extent that you trust Me. Every problem can teach you something, transforming you little by little into the masterpiece I created you to be."

Numerous scriptures remind us that God is the ultimate Life Guard and His purpose for allowing flood waters in our lives is not to stand back and watch us drown. Nor does He want us to flail about in the rising depths, sputtering and gasping for breath in defeat. He longs for us to rest in Him -- trusting Him to keep us afloat and bring us to the safety of dry land --"...*He drew me out of many waters...the Lord was my support. He also brought me out into a broad place; He delivered me because He delighted in me*" Psalm 18:16, 19.

I'll be the first to admit I don't have all the answers to cultivating peace and joy when our journey takes us through the flood. It was a source of great sorrow for all of us to watch Mama's sadness and struggle during her last two years. But, the sovereign God who created you and me and every inch of floodwater, has a plan for every soggy minute we must endure before we're back on dry land. I won't pretend it's easy -- in fact, you can be sure it is often unbelievably hard, but God does have a plan and, believe it or not, getting wet now and then is the best way to grow fruit for His glory. A well-watered garden produces the best flowers and fruit. Let Him splash joy and peace into your life in His way and His time -- the eternal results will be a thing of beauty.

Mama would not have chosen the path she stumbled along at the end of her life, but when she took her last breath on earth and opened her eyes in heaven, the joy and peace awaiting her there ended her floodwaters in a heartbeat. *"To be absent from the body is to be present with the Lord."* God delivered her out of many waters and brought her to the broad place that had been prepared for her before the foundation of the world.

"Shout with joy to God, all the earth! Sing the glory of His name; make His praise glorious! Say to God, 'How awesome are your deeds! So great is your power...' He turned the sea into dry land, they passed through the waters on foot...For you, O God, tested us; you refined us like silver...we went through fire and water, but you brought us to a place of abundance...God has surely listened and heard my voice in prayer. Praise be to God" from Psalm 66.

Photo: I took the picture of my mother's hands when she was 90 years old. She was such a prayer warrior. Her hands rest on her mother's Bible – my grandmother. Mother died only two months before her 94th birthday and was immediately in the joyous presence of Jesus. SJB

SANDRA

Not every story in this book is one of tragedy. A few of the stories contain challenges that try the soul, and show how God came through and resolved those trying issues in His own miraculous, wonder-working way. Mine is such a story:

For as long as I can remember, all I wanted to be was a wife and mother – that was my most important goals in life. When I was twenty-one years old, my first goal was reached and I was married to my dear husband Larry.

Two years after we were married, I quit my job as a legal secretary, and settled down to being a homemaker. I'd worked for seven years as a secretary. Now I was free to begin seeking my second goal – being a mother. Three more years passed and we still seemed no closer to having the longed-for baby we'd been hoping for. My arms ached for a baby of my own.

We called our local social service office and requested an application to adopt. At that time, we knew several couples who'd adopted and others who were in the process of adopting. In some cases, things had not worked out so well for the families and the children they'd adopted wreaked havoc in the home. So – we knew it was not always a simple thing to "adopt and live happily ever after." It would need to be God's will for our family – not just our own will.

Months passed since I'd called to request an application be mailed to us. During those months, I called several more times and each time, the person assured me the papers would soon arrive. We began to think perhaps it was not God's will for us to adopt. Although we wanted a baby, we really didn't want to go out of God's will.

I love the way Moses put it, *"If Your Presence does not go with us, do not bring us up from here"* Exodus 33:15.

It was imperative for us to know if it was God's will for us to adopt a baby. And so – I put a fleece before my heavenly Father. In His love, He answered my need for assurance and, as He did with Gideon,

He gave me the full assurance miracle that I needed – and to this day, it has continued to bolster my faith.

One morning, several months after we'd requested the application, I prayed to God, saying, "Lord, if it is your will for us to adopt a baby, let the application be in the mailbox today. If it is not your will, then don't let it be there."

I felt the need to come boldly before the Lord and He honored my request.

As I prayerfully walked toward the mailbox that afternoon, I admit to being nervous. Then, when I opened the box and saw the manila envelope from the social service office, I was one happy young woman! I was happy not only because God was going to give us a baby through adoption, but also because the Creator of the entire universe had stooped down to beautifully answer our great need for assurance.

God later confirmed this first assurance with a second miracle. Two months after God blessed us with a baby boy through adoption, He blessed us with the long-awaited pregnancy that would give us a daughter nine months later. God waited until we had our precious son before He sent our precious daughter.

As a result of these two miraculous confirmations that God wanted us to adopt Nathan, we have never doubted for a minute that he is indeed our true son, chosen for us by God from his birth. Such assurance is especially helpful when you go through the difficult years of adolescents (:

Twenty years ago, I wrote a story describing some of my feelings on the day our son arrived. Here is an excerpt from, "A Treasure Without Price," published in *Chicken Soup for the Mother's Soul* (copyright 1997):

"I had waited nearly five years for this moment. Five years enduring the empty arms of childlessness, the baby showers for someone else, and the well-meaning question from friends, "Are you pregnant yet?"

I longed for a baby of my own, and at last it was happening. Our baby was due to arrive anytime. My husband and I waited with bated breath, our hearts pounding with anticipation. Soon, he would be here – soon! We had been told it was a boy. A son of our very own. What joy!

Years ago, before we knew of the long painful journey ahead in our quest for a child, I had chosen a boy's name. For some reason, we had never been able to settle on a girl's name, but the boy's name had come quickly, with no hesitation and no second thoughts. Our son would be Nathan Andrew, meaning "Gift from God" in the Hebrew language. I was unaware of the name's meaning when I first began sounding it out on my tongue. I just liked the way it flowed – the fine, masculine ring it produced in my ear. I chose my son's name long before he was ever conceived, when he was still a desire deep in my heart. Once I discovered the significance of the name, I was doubly pleased. How fitting a name for such a precious gift from God.

Now we waited for Nathan Andrew to arrive. The painful months and years we had endured would soon become a dim memory.

A car drove up and parked in front of the house. We pressed close to the window, eagerly waiting as a woman stepped out of the car with a blanket-wrapped baby carrier. As she walked up the sidewalk, I held my breath, my eyes never leaving the shrouded bundle she carried. I would soon hold my baby in my arms. Yes, God had chosen to answer our prayer through adoption.

The scene was suddenly thrown into slow motion, and questions flashed through my mind with the speed of light. What of the girl who had borne him? What of the young man who had fathered him? What were they doing on this day?

I thought of this young girl, ten years younger than I. She was somewhere in this city, recuperating from the birth of her baby that was no longer her baby. After nine months of waiting, she had given life to a little boy. After five years of waiting, we were taking that little boy and giving him the life he deserved. We would be the mother and father who would love him, providing for his physical, emotional and spiritual needs in ways that a young girl was not yet capable of doing.

With tears in my eyes, I silently thanked a stranger whose baby would become my own. At peril to herself, she had carried and nourished him in her body, she had endured the pain of delivery, and would carry the scars of childbirth until her dying day. And then, she had given him to me.

I was his mother now, and for the rest of his life. I slipped the blanket from its tent-like perch on the handle of the baby carrier and stared into the face of my son. Big, gray eyes fringed with thick black lashes solemnly stared back at me. I touched the tiny, perfectly formed fingers and toes. He was beautiful!

With heartfelt words of gratitude, I whispered "Thank you!" not only to God for answering our prayers and sending us a son, but also to a girl I would never meet. A girl whose gift was a treasure without price. Thank you."

Photo: This is one of my favorite pictures. Nathan had fallen asleep in my arms on the way home from church and Larry snapped this photo in our driveway. This was, of course, before the days of required car seats for little ones.

ELIZABETH

~Elizabeth Shares her Story:

"I was saved at the age of four years old when I knelt at my bed beside my mother and asked Jesus to come into my heart. I have fond memories of my sister and I gluing pages of Bible characters onto flannel and cutting them out for our mother to use in her Child Evangelism Bible class for teachers. Our mother would use the figures to tell us the story before she told it to a roomful of teachers. God's power to rescue His people became evident to me as a child through these flannel board characters.

Both my parents loved the Lord, and they stressed scripture memorization. When we woke up each morning, we prayed from Psalm 5:3, *"My voice shalt Thou hear in the morning, oh, LORD; in the morning will I direct my prayer unto Thee and will look up."*

As we slipped under the covers at night, we prayed from Psalm 4:8, *"I will both lay me down in peace, and sleep; for Thou LORD only makes me dwell in safety."*

By the time I reached my mid-forties, I had a lovely home, a wonderful Christian husband, two fine teenage children, and a fulfilling career in teaching – everything I'd ever dreamed of. Life was good and the happy verses I'd learned as a child resonated with the joy of "peace and safety" I saw in God's promises.

But then, something happened and those promises of God took on new meaning. The new chapter I was stepping into would require believing God's promises with eyes of faith – meaning, to believe in something we can no longer see with our eyes. I had to mix His promises with faith and cement them into my daily life – hour by hour, minute by minute.

At the age of 44 years old, I began feeling occasional weakness and tingling in my arms and legs. On one family vacation to the Blue Ridge Mountains, I wondered why a walk up a hill should be so difficult.

"C'mon, Mom, you can do it. We'll push!" my two kids said. And with those words, my husband and kids got behind my 110-pound, 5'3" frame and gave me the boost I needed to get up the hill.

As the months passed, however, late-in-the-day foot drags became more frequent and sometimes I fell for no reason.

For the first few years, symptoms were so sporadic I shrugged them off with excuses like being over-tired or over-stressed or just being a klutz. The symptoms indicating that I was living with a neurological disease appeared so gradually that neither I nor close friends noticed them.

Visits to general practitioners didn't help, especially when they sloughed it off as probably just being in my head.

When I began dropping things and could no longer lift my arm to write on the chalkboard at school, and was having difficulty walking the length of the hall, I realized I needed to seek help. The math teacher at the school where I taught had been newly diagnosed with MS that year, and I noticed that her leg was dragging as she walked just like mine did sometimes. I got the name of her neurologist and called him.

At first glance, the doctor didn't think my condition was serious. He told me not to worry, which was a definite relief, but then test results proved otherwise and a few days later, he called me with the news, saying, "You do have lesions on your brain and spinal cord that indicate multiple sclerosis," adding, "There's no cure."

In that moment, pictures of two women I knew who had been diagnosed with MS entered my mind: Harriett, who was going to leave her teaching position, and my friend Susan, who had stopped coming to church. Both women were on the weekly prayer request list at church. Surely, God did not have this journey as a plan for my life too!

As the doctor talked about possible medication to slow down the progression, the words, "'MS, interferon injections, no cure,' were penetrating my mind. What happened to the lingering words from the doctor three days before suggesting that he saw nothing to worry about? I was suddenly filled with fear at what lay ahead of me.

Within the year, I needed a cane to help me walk down the hall at the school where I taught and two years later, a four-wheeled walker.

At first, after a few hundred feet, I needed to sit and rest. As time went by, that distance grew shorter. One day, as I sat down to rest and saw how much further I had to go, I began to sob as I realized how the distance was closing in. I soon had to use a scooter to get down the long corridor at school during the four years that I clung to doing the job I loved.

Going from using a walker to the wheelchair was necessary but a huge defeat for me. My world shrunk from having limited control to not being able to drive, relying on someone to fix my meals and assist with bathing and personal grooming. I had lost my ability to cook, clean house, grocery shop – all the things that a wife would normally do.

When I began to lose my ability to walk – first with a cane and later using a walker and wheelchair, I grieved each loss and cried easily when I was unable to do the things I used to do so readily. I was never angry with God, but I did become both frustrated and angry when I could not open a jar or reach an item from my wheelchair. Having to ask for help was – and continues to be frustrating.

Although I was saved as a child, I was still what I would call -- a baby Christian. As I increased prayer and Bible study in my daily life, my faith grew stronger. I knew that God had the power to heal me, but in the meantime I needed a steady diet of His Word to give me strength.

I have learned to trust God regardless of how difficult the journey becomes with an illness that has robbed me of all of my ability to live independently. Giving up my right to control where I go or when I do things has made me submit to accepting help from caregivers – my husband and daughter.

Leaving my job was one of the hardest things I've ever done. I'd wanted to be a teacher since I was a small child. When I was little, I lined my dolls and stuffed animals up in front of a chalk board and taught them the numbers and ABCs that my older sister had taught me.

I'd been a teacher for 29 years, teaching English and Latin. I loved my students and loved helping open their understanding in these subjects. I asked everyone at church to pray for me to be able to continue teaching, telling them, 'It is my whole identity.' They would nod and promise to pray – and all the while, my heart was breaking and I was scared.

On one occasion, I asked a former missionary to pray and added the part about it being my identity. He kindly reminded me that my identity was not with my job, but was with my heavenly Father. That gentle reminder helped me admit both to him and to God that yes, my sole identity was not in my job as a teacher, nor in the wheelchair in which I now sat, but rather in my relationship as a daughter to my God and King, and my identity as His beloved child is eternally secure.

That year I prepared to leave my job. It was time. Even with a left foot accelerator installed, I had problems safely getting myself to and from school.

How would I fill my days, I still wondered?

I smile now as I remember those times of uncertainty. God took care of filling my time just as he had given me peace about leaving my beloved career. First, I began praying each week in the prayer garden of our church with a friend who loves to pray. Then, I was asked to teach a Latin class at the Christian school two mornings each week.

In recent years when I had to give up driving completely, several home school parents asked me to teach Latin to their child at my own home. Wow, God! I thought. You gave back to me double -- as you did to Job after his years of great distress. All the years in public school I had not been able to bring in scripture when I taught. I wanted so badly to use the Latin Bible in my lessons but never could. Now, I had parents asking me to use scripture.

Yes, God has blessed me so much during the years my health has steadily declined, but it has not been easy for either me or my husband Dick. He retired to take care of me. He would tell you that this disease is his disease as well.

In the last ten years I have lost all ability to use my right leg and right hand. I was right-handed and have learned to eat with my left hand. Writing and typing have been more challenging. I can only move my arm up to waist level.

With my left hand losing strength now, I wonder how long I will enjoy its use. The Lord has brought me so far in accepting what I cannot do, but I pray that not being able to feed myself will not be added to the list.

God's continual supply of sustaining grace has amazed me throughout each new loss of being able to do for myself. For the past 12 years I have taught a ladies' Bible class at church. God teaches me so many truths to apply to my daily walk with Him as I prepare to teach the lesson. We study a different book of the Bible every quarter and the treasures I find in God's word astound me.

I see that my willingness to let God use me can -- in my wheelchair -- encourage them to keep relying on God as they go through difficult circumstances in their lives. 'Don't give up,' I say to them. 'Let God use your storms to glorify your all-sufficient unchanging God -- to spread the fragrance of Him everywhere,'

Friends still ask *how I do it*. They see me seated in my scooter as I zip down a church hallway or maneuver around shoppers in Wal-Mart aisles. The picture of seeing me walking has not been blotted from their memories.

They still remember walking with me to the parking lot after work or meeting at a local restaurant before multiple sclerosis robbed me of that luxury. They remember the woman who met them at the local fitness center twice a week or who signed them up to walk with her in the ten-mile walk for a local charity.

These are things I remember as well. If I let myself dwell on all I've lost (as Satan would have me do), I could become even more helpless. I do have times of discouragement. There have been times filled with much grief and pain. Times when I've said to God, 'I don't know if I can keep doing this. It's just so hard!'

It's in times like these that I put on praise music and just silently listen to the message of the awesomeness of God. I recently read that if you scramble the letters of the word LISTEN, you have the word SILENT. Psalm 46:10 reminds me to be still – *'Be still, and know that I am God; I will be exalted among the nations, I will be exalted in the earth!'*

I could dwell on what I've lost, or rejoice in what I've gained. I think of the sweet fellowship I enjoy with the Lord now and recall that I did not have this intimacy with Him when I was physically a whole person with no sign of illness. The Lord has filled all of the hollow places with his blessings to use me to teach and share with women of all ages. I sometimes ask myself, did it really take this to teach me that my soul is more important to God than my body?

God blesses me with simple joys as well. During the spring, I have a bluebird family in the bird house outside my kitchen window. They bring me immense joy as I watch them and consider the words of Matthew 6:26 that tell me to *'look at the birds of the air; they do not sow or reap or store away in barns, and yet your heavenly Father feeds them.'*

Here are a few of the promises that reassure me of who God is and how I do not need to doubt His provisions for me:

-The Faithful God: *'He is the Rock, his works are perfect, and all his ways are just. A faithful God who does no wrong, upright and just is he'* Deuteronomy 32:4 NIV.

-The source of my strength: *'He will be a spirit of justice to him who sits in judgment, a source of strength to those who turn back the battle at the gate'* Isaiah 28:6 NIV.

-God, my Rock: *'I say to God my rock...'* Psalm 42:9 NIV.

-My confidence: *'For you have been my hope, O Sovereign Lord, my confidence since my youth'* Psalm 71:5 NIV.

-My Hiding Place: *'You are my hiding place; you will protect me from trouble and surround me with songs of deliverance'* Psalm 32:7 NIV.

-My Dwelling Place: *'Lord, you have been our dwelling place throughout all generations'* Psalm 90:1 NIV.

-My Help and Shield: *We wait in hope for the Lord; he is our help and our shield'* Psalm 33:20 NIV.

These are just a few of God's promises that restore me when I wonder if I can keep going. Satan's attacks of doubt can sometimes cause me to think, 'This is too hard, or You should not teach a ladies class when you keep dropping pencils and papers on the floor. You can't even write on the board as the other teachers do.' This is when I remind myself of God's promises and counter the doubts with what God says.

I used to look at women in wheelchairs and think, I could never live in a situation like that, or I would pray that I would never have to suffer in that way. With God all things are possible to those who believe. I now believe -- not in my ability to cope with daily being in a wheelchair or of not being able to even get in or out or bed by myself, but in the God of heaven and earth who daily provides me with His strength to face even more loss from the progression of this disease or loss in any other area of my life.

I daily fight the fear of losing my husband, the love of my life as well as my faithful caregiver, but the God who says 'I change not' assures me that He will be faithful to provide for me even if I have to experience the loss of my love of over four decades of my life.

As degeneration in the myelin continues to rob me of my mobility, the Lord regenerates my soul and spirit to lift up my heart daily in praise to him for his sustaining grace, and to glorify Him for the work He is doing in my life.

I have my mother's Bible in which she wrote notes in every margin; some of them she signed with her initials 'E.S.B.' I prayed that God would give me her love for Jesus when she died. My daughter tells me I sound just like Grandma when I share verses with her. God is so faithful to give us more and more of his love. All it takes is to be thirsty; I was and still am.

One of the scriptures that's at the top of my favorites list is found in Isaiah 26:3-4 NIV: *'You will keep in perfect peace him whose mind is steadfast, because he trusts in you. / Trust in the LORD forever, for the LORD, the LORD, is the Rock eternal.'* Beside this verse I have written my name -- Elizabeth Walker Peterson -- who trusts in her Rock eternal for her present and future years."

-Photo: Courtesy photo of Elizabeth

ELEANOR

"God moves in mysterious ways; His wonders to perform" -- these first two lines of the well-known hymn written by William Cowper in 1773 perfectly describe the way our extraordinary God worked in the life of a sister in Christ when He met a great need in the lives of she and her children.

-Eleanor shares her story:

"After several years as a single mother with two small children, I began to realize that with God's help, I could actually make it on my own. It had not been easy to get to that point. I started out that year with little confidence in raising two children by myself. Many times during those first years of struggle, I felt like I just couldn't do it. How could I possibly continue to support myself and two children? At such times, God always reached down and picked me up. He was always there for me, and I learned to fully rely on His help for everything.

I'd been working as a Head Teller at a Savings & Loan Association for four years when I began to think about buying a house for me and my children. I wanted to make things as normal as possible for my young son and daughter, so I thought we needed our own house and a yard for them to play in. Every Sunday for months, I poured through the real estate section of the newspaper looking for just the right house for my family. I'd already spent time riding around neighborhoods and talking with people, checking out different locations in the area to see which would be best for our situation. After doing research, I decided on one particular area that had modest homes, and looked like it was a good place to raise my children. It was affordable and was close to my family, my church and my workplace.

As weeks and months passed and I'd called realtors about several advertised listings, I realized what a massive step this was for me to take. How could I handle all these decisions on my own? How could I be sure I'd be able to make the mortgage payments every month? Where would I even get enough money for a down payment and all the closing expenses? What did I know about being a homeowner? How could I possibly make such a long-term commitment?

I began to doubt my decision to buy a house on my own, and I was becoming stressed over the entire situation. In desperation (not sure why we always wait until we're desperate to ask for God's help!), I turned my needs and my doubts completely over to God. I told Him if it was meant for me to buy a house He would have to bring the house to me. I was done trying to work this thing out on my own. God knew what I needed better than I did anyway.

I can't tell you what a load was taken off my shoulders when I cried out to the Lord, laid my needs at His feet – and left them there. A peace came over me. I was ready to accept whatever God had in store for me. The verse that I held dear to my heart – and still do to this day is: *"Trust in the Lord with all thine heart; and lean not unto thine own understanding. In all thy ways acknowledge Him, and He shall direct thy paths"* Proverbs 3:5-6 KJV.

A few weeks after I turned my needs over to God, I was at work when a woman I'd known since we were teenagers came into the office to put in an application for a new house she and her husband were buying. Looking back, I can see the hand of God working at every turn – even causing my old friend to choose our office to come in and get her loan. During our conversation, I asked about the house they were selling and she told me they'd decided to sell it themselves – which meant no realtor fees. I asked about the location of the house and – yes – you guessed it – the house was located in the exact area I had chosen as a good place for me and my children to live. I was beginning to get excited.

I didn't waste any time. A few days later, I went and looked at the property. As soon as I saw the well-kept house, the fenced-in backyard and all the children playing around the neighborhood, I felt like I'd come home. I loved it! In my heart, I felt this was where God was leading me.

Now keep in mind, I had $2,000 in my savings account and that was all I had to my name. I knew to make this happen, God would have to provide the rest. However, at this point He had brought the house to me just as I'd prayed – surely He would take care of the rest.

My first step was to sign a contract for the house and pray for God's hand to work out the multitude of details that would be necessary for this to work.
Next, I filled out a loan application at the Savings & Loan where I worked (hmmm…I wonder if God had this whole thing planned when He led me to take this job at a Savings & Loan company?).
A few days after I applied for the mortgage loan, our Vice President called me into his office. He told me that at my income level, I didn't qualify for the loan amount needed to purchase the house – but, that he would okay the loan anyway. He said he had every confidence that I would pay back the mortgage. I was stunned. This Vice President was a bachelor, older in age, very conservative in conducting business -- and he was not a Christian. I knew this was truly a God thing.

Next on the list of miracles was a discount in the interest rate I was qualified to receive because I worked at the company. When my employer showed me what my monthly payment would be, I was elated. I'd never dreamed it would be that affordable.
Closing costs for a loan can be steep. I wondered if my savings would cover the costs. I'm not sure why I was worried, hadn't God been going before me every step of the way?
When it came time to take care of the necessary survey of the property, I asked my manager if he would call the survey company and tell them I was a single mother, and could they give me a break. I knew that he had just closed on a loan himself and the surveyor had only charged him half-price for his survey. When the invoice for the survey arrived in the office, it was stamped "Paid in full." I remember my manager saying, "That God of yours must follow you all around." What a witness this was turning out to be!

Our loving God is so giving. He tied up His beautiful gift package to me with a big bow when one of the attorneys who did work for the Savings & Loan agreed to close my loan for free.

The first day we moved in, my daughter met a girl across the street that was just her age. The next day there were several other girls her age that came over to play. I was excited for my children that we could put down roots and call this 'our home.'

When I'd prayed and told God that if He wanted me to have a house, He'd have to bring it to me – He worked out every detail and did that very thing – so beautifully! I'm reminded of the verse in Ephesians 3:20: *"Now to Him who is able to do immeasurably more than all we ask or imagine, according to His power that is at work within us, to Him be glory in the church and in Christ Jesus throughout all generations, forever and ever!"*

Since that day so many years ago, I can honestly say I never worried about making my house payments as a single parent because I knew God had put His stamp of approval on this transaction.

What my manager didn't realize was that God did indeed follow me all around.

-Photo: Courtesy picture of Eleanor's son at the home God gave them.

LORA

One day I was reading Facebook, and I saw an entry that brought tears to my eyes. It was written by a young woman who'd been a playmate to my daughter Holly throughout their childhoods. Our families had been good friends, and we'd been next door neighbors at one time. I'd not seen Lora for more than 20 years, but I knew her story well.

Here's what I read on Lora's Facebook page on May 18, 2015: *I know most of you will understand this, but some of you won't...but I just have to say how Amazing our God is...how He has healed my heart towards Nicholas, and how thankful I am for His mercy to me! All Glory To HIM!*

As soon as I saw this wonderful testimony of forgiveness for something many might consider unforgivable, I felt God letting me know that her story needed to be included in this book. Praise God, He spoke to Lora's heart at the very same time, and told her she needed to write her story. He brought us together, and she now shares her heart with you.

~Lora Shares her Story:

"I was fourteen years old when it happened. My brother Will was thirteen. It was nine days before Christmas, and we were excited about the upcoming holidays. A decorated Christmas tree stood tall in one corner of the living room, with lots of colorful wrapped packages underneath.

That Friday morning when we pulled away from the house to go to school, I was wearing my cheerleading uniform, and we were all talking about the basketball game that evening and the things we planned to do over the weekend. Momma was a business teacher (math and typing) at the Christian school we attended, and she drove us to school every day. It's hard to believe that morning was so ordinary when only a few hours later life as we knew it would be ripped apart.

It was at the beginning of my morning Bible class. Most of our classes were held in trailers, and from the back of the classroom, we saw police cars on the other side of the building...sticking out from the side. I thought nothing of it because my previous school was robbed all the time, and I thought that was what had happened here too.

It wasn't long before someone from administration came around to the classrooms and told us all to meet in the sanctuary. I remember goofing around with my friends on the way into the church and even when we got inside. We didn't know what was going on. We'd heard nothing about a shooting.

I don't remember really asking for Mom, but one of the teachers told me she'd gone with another teacher to the hospital - which made sense to me. A little later, another teacher told me that she'd gone to a different hospital with Mr. Marino, the male teacher who'd been shot.

At that point, I still wasn't worried.

Then, someone from administration pulled my brother Will and I out into the hallway and a few minutes later told us to return to our seats. It wasn't until years later that I learned the reason they'd told us to return to our seats so quickly. They were bringing mom's body out of the trailer, and we could have witnessed that through the glass doors in the foyer of the sanctuary.

A few minutes later someone called us back again and this time took us to the pastor's study. That's when they told us that my mother was dead - killed by another student. I really don't remember what they specifically said - memories of that moment are hazy. I do remember sitting on the couch with my brother, crying and waiting for our father to arrive. While we were waiting for our father to get there, we went back into the sanctuary and hugged pretty much everyone in there.

The media was already out in the parking lot, and the administration was attempting to get the two of us out of the building before the media knew who we were. They were asking parents of our friends if we could go home with them. This was before the common cell phone, and we still had not spoken to our father. My brother went ahead and went with a family, but I stayed to wait for dad. Once he got there, we hugged and sat there crying together for a while before deciding where I would go for the evening. My father was in shock, but he had a funeral to plan. I'm sure he was glad to know we were in safe hands. It all seemed so unreal.

The next few days were busy with a Viewing on Saturday night (I didn't go because I didn't want to see anyone, and I didn't want to remember momma that way), a Memorial Service Sunday evening, and the funeral on Monday.

What does a young teenage girl remember about such events? Here's what I remember:

I knew one of the outfits I was supposed to be getting for Christmas – it was a black and white outfit. I talked dad into letting me open the gift so I could wear the outfit to the funeral. We arrived at the church and went in a door that is usually not used. I had two close friends who sat with me at the funeral. The sanctuary was literally wall to wall people and the media. My dad's stomach growled during the service, and we got a chuckle out of it.

Several people got up to testify about their memories of momma, and *People Need the Lord* was sung by one of her favorite godly women.

The coffin...weird...my mother was in there. I just sat and stared at it.... After the service, I remember everyone staring at us as we walked out and back to the car. Before we pulled away, a reporter stuck his head in the car window and asked us a question. I don't know what he asked, but I do remember saying some unkind words to him.

After the graveside service, we went back to our house and there continued to be many people. The flowers...there were flowers everywhere...and food – lots of it! There were tons of people...even people standing in my closet talking.

Eventually everyone left, and we didn't know what to do. It was such a lost feeling.

What do you do when this was all you knew? So, back to school we went – the same school where my mother was so recently murdered. The school kept the trailers where these tragedies had taken place. I literally walked past the trailer where my mother was killed every day several times a day. I had mixed feelings about the school keeping the trailer. I actually wanted to peek inside and see if there was anything left from that day - anything left of my momma.

I thought about it literally every time I walked past - my mom died in there. It was extremely surreal.

The trailers are now gone, and my son (who goes to that same school) and I have walked past that grassy area many times. I pointed out to him that it was where Grandma Karen was killed. We even had a small picnic there one year on his birthday during school hours.

I wasn't the only one who had issues with the trailers. The students who had been shot at also had to go back into the same trailer and see bullet holes in the walls. Interestingly, the school offered counseling to those students who had been involved in the shooting, but no one ever said anything to Will and I about whether we needed to speak with someone.

What would I have said if I'd spoken to a counselor back then? Would I have pointed out the incredible loss I was feeling – a loss that would continue to haunt me throughout the next 25 years of my life?

I would ask, why MY mother? Why her? My mom was all we knew. We knew and loved our father too, but we didn't spend the time with him that we did with her. Momma was the one who led me to the Lord when I was five years old. She was always there for us - she took us to school, took us to practices, took us to church. She always knew if we were in trouble – and handled it. She was a great mother, teacher, daughter, sister, wife...so, why her, I would ask?

Karen

My mom was not even the target of this shooting – she just got in the way. Nicholas came to school that morning with a loaded gun and a few homemade bombs. He was intent on killing a particular student who'd been bullying him for the past year and also a teacher who he believed had encouraged the bullying. As Nicholas went from trailer to trailer searching for his targets, he happened into my mom's classroom where she sat at her desk alone. He shot her twice – once in the hand and then in the chest. He then continued his hunt. One other teacher, Mr. Marino, was wounded while others fled flying bullets until his gun jammed, and he was tackled by another teacher and stopped.

One of my first thoughts about the tragedy was, why did Mr. Marino get to live? He too was shot twice, but he lived. I would see him at school and think, 'Why did he get to live and my momma didn't?'

I cried myself to sleep many, many times! I guess the hardest time I had was once I was married. She wasn't there to talk to about 'married life'. I would just cry and talk to God and continue to ask Him 'Why?'

Over the years, I've come to a possible answer to the question, 'Why her?' Everyone who knew my mother, knew she was a Christian. There was no question about it. If any child/student had been killed that day, there most likely would have been a question about their walk with our Lord, but not with her. She sacrificed her life so that other students - her students - could have a relationship with Christ. This includes the young man who killed her. I know that she would want him to accept Christ as his Lord and Savior as well.

Have I experienced bitterness over the loss of my mother? Oh, yes...bitterness. Oh, how I hated going almost anywhere and seeing a daughter with her mother out shopping! It is still something I kind of struggle with. She wasn't there for me to pick out my Junior or Senior prom dresses, or Homecoming dress – and most importantly, my wedding dress. She wasn't there when I got my driver's license, when I graduated from high school, for my birthdays or my brother's birthdays, the birth of my son, and all the "regular" days that I have had since she was killed. How I missed that I never got to call her up and tell her about a new outfit or a sale....nothing.

There is a mother and daughter in my neighborhood who go walking on my street almost every evening. I stopped going walking when they were walking because I just had this yearning to have my mother there to walk with me. Shortly after changing my walking schedule, I started attending a new church, and guess who was there? Yes, this mother and daughter attended that church too.

I eventually got up the nerve to speak to these two women and tell them a little about my story. After I shared about my great loss, they could not hug my neck fast enough. They were touched by my story, and we all cried together. They also invited me to start walking with them.

I was angry with God for a little bit...probably not as long as most people would have been. I knew it wasn't God who did this, but then I also knew God could have stopped it from happening. My anger was definitely geared toward the student who had pulled the trigger - Nicholas.

For many, many years I wanted Nicholas, the boy who killed momma – raped in prison, beaten up, just physically hurt! I wanted him to hurt for all of the pain I felt nearly every day.

Since I was a Christian, as I grew older, I knew it was wrong to hate Nicholas...for any reason. So, many years ago I started praying that God would change my heart toward him. I called my brother about it because even though I had prayed about it, I still didn't feel like I'd been able to completely forgive Nicholas. Will wisely pointed out that we are still human - and God knows this.

I wanted to be able to forgive him regardless of how he felt toward us, and why he had killed her. God is gracious and in December 2013, I found out that Nicholas had sent a letter years earlier to one of the teachers of the school and told her he was sorry and asked for forgiveness.

Once I found out that Nicholas was remorseful, my heart softened even more towards him. I tried to contact the prison to go see him...which I discovered, you can't just do...you can't just "swing by" and chat. I had watched too much *Law & Order*.

My brother and I applied for a Victim Offender Dialogue (VOD). Over the next few months, we went through the process required to meet with Nicholas – each of us meeting with a therapist – back and forth. Nicholas honestly thought we wanted to meet with him to physically hurt him...attack him. The therapist assured him we were not there to harm him!

During the months of therapy, my heart continued to heal and soften towards him. I just kept thinking Christ died on the cross for me...He sent His son for me...He sent His son for Nicholas too! I would think about my own son and how hard it would be if he had done something this violent...would I still love him....of course I would!

So, when we finally met Nicholas, on April 13, 2014, I wanted to give him a big ole' hug and let him know that we were here to show Christ's love and forgiveness to him. Instead, I just sat there trying to smile, to offer him reassurance that it was going to be okay. Ironically, Will broke down crying...which I loved 'cause he rarely cried....you know, men! Even though I'd done most of my crying in the therapy sessions, we all ended up crying during the course of the meeting. It was just such a great meeting! There was an empty chair in the assistant warden's office where we were meeting, and I told Will that Jesus was sitting there with us.

I was so thankful that we were able to meet with him and hear his heart. As a mother, my heart actually breaks for him. This terrible mistake he made at such a young age of sixteen years old. Oh, the stupid mistakes we make as teenagers.

Nicholas and I are e-mailing and writing each other! Since he is in prison, I even visited his mother on Mother's Day for him. Never in a million years would I have thought I would have this much love for him! I care for him, and I want to see him become a Christian and use this tragedy for good in his life as well.

One of the things I've discovered over the years is that My God was there the entire time. He was waiting on me! It was not until I was married - in my twenties - that I really started focusing my life back on Christ. However, I had a turn of events in my career just last year, and the Lord became even more 'real' to me then. I honestly hate how I had not been this close to Him all these years! All that I missed out on from Him!

I say to any sister or brother in need - God is there! Turn to Him, cry out to Him! He wants to love and comfort you! I also urge you to love your parents...and all of the clichés…. Make every moment with your family count! Tell them how much you love them! Realize that there is more to life than 'things.' Spend time with your family and the ones you love!

I am thankful for the time I had with my Momma Karen; thankful that she taught me how to make homemade Stromboli, my love for cheering and dancing; thankful that she taught me how to shave my legs; thankful that I saw her on her knees with a Bible in front of her praying for our family, and thankful she showed me how a Christian should live! I miss ya momma! I have so much to tell ya! Thank God that I know I will see you again!"

Photo: Courtesy photo of Karen taken a few years before she went up to heaven.

SANDY

Sandy's story begins in 2007 when her 39 year old husband was diagnosed with liver disease. Scott never drank alcohol, smoked or used drugs. He loved to surf, bike, fly stunt kites and spend time with his family, yet here he was -- a seemingly healthy young man with cirrhosis of the liver. Two years earlier when their daughter Paige was five years old, she was diagnosed with Type 1 diabetes and had to begin insulin therapy. On top of that, when Sandy began having joint and muscle pain, tests revealed she had rheumatoid arthritis.

When asked by a friend how she managed to cope, she said, "God saw that my plate was full, so He gave me a platter."

Although these three physical conditions were challenging, symptoms were controlled by medication, the family adjusted and life settled back to a fairly normal rhythm. Scott had a job he enjoyed, and Sandy was a teacher at a nearby Christian school where their two young daughters attended. They were active in their church, and were just managing to keep their heads above water with added costs of medication and doctor's visits.

Then, just after school started in 2012, Scott's liver became symptomatic. He needed frequent treatments to keep his liver functioning and in March 2013 he was put on the transplant list at a university hospital three hours from their home. His struggle ended when he stepped into heaven exactly 24 months later.

During this entire saga, Sandy kept friends and family updated on their situation via regular emails. Within this story, Sandy's own words from her emails will speak for her. I've used email excerpts, hoping you will feel the impact of Sandy and Scott's story by reading it as if in real time. This has been a long journey for them, but as Sandy frequently wrote, "None of this is a surprise to God and He will not leave us."

When they discovered Scott's need for a new liver, Sandy wrote: "We serve a mighty God who knows exactly what is needed and when. I am asking that my friends and prayer warriors join us in bombarding Heaven on my husband's behalf. To be more specific, we are praying for ultimate healing - whether it be through a transplant or through God's awesome power. Either way, we will give God the glory!"

The same week that Sandy sent in papers requesting a liver transplant for Scott, their seven-year old daughter Sidney became sick and was diagnosed with Type 1 diabetes. Now, both Paige and Sidney would need insulin therapy. Sandy's next email read: "Although we would not choose this path for either of our girls, we know that God has great things in store for both of them!"

At 1:30am on April 8, 2013, they received a phone call from the hospital that a liver was available for Scott and they should immediately begin the three hour journey from their home to the hospital. Surgery was scheduled for noon. They were excited and nervous.

At 11am, while preparing for surgery, they were informed the liver meant for Scott was unusable. Sandy wrote: "This was a disappointment at first, but we know God has a plan. Your prayers are not in vain. God allowed the surgeons to notice the 'issues' *before* Scott was on the operating table. In God's Hands. Pray Scott does not lose his place on the list and we may be back very soon."

Little did Sandy know when she wrote those words that it would be more than four months before they received another call that a liver for Scott was available.

The end of June, Scott's health improved just enough to knock him to a lower number on the transplant list. Sandy felt as if a balloon had burst inside her. She wrote: "When our nurse coordinator told me this on Wednesday, I burst into tears! I felt like we were at #1 or #2 for so long with no transplant, now it is not even in view for us. After I calmed down, I reminded her (and myself) that we are believers and that none of this is a surprise to God. HE has Scott's life in His hands and we will continue to trust in Him. In our opinion, God is either healing Scott's liver, or He has another plan that we can't see.

"This week I was reminded of Acts 15:18, '*Known to God from eternity, are all His works.*'"

"Honestly, I have really struggled lately with God's plan. I keep praying and I know there are people all over the world who are praying for our family, but at times it seems that He is not listening. I was reminded this week that HE IS! Our Sunday School teacher sent me some verses in John 15. *"If you remain in me and my words remain in you, ask whatever you wish, and it will be done for you. This is to my Father's glory, that you bear much fruit, showing yourselves to be my disciples."* God WILL heal Scott, but will do it in HIS time and so our Father will get the glory. In the meantime, we will be faithful and continue to abide in Him. Scott and I are the only Christian examples many of these doctors and nurses will see."

August 16 – 9:45 in the morning, they receive a call from the nurse coordinator at the hospital, "Sandy, I have some good news. We have a liver for your husband."

Sandy wrote: "I was shocked and replied, *'Seriously?!? You really are serious?'* I thought, why did I question God like that? I had just prayed about 30 minutes before and asked Him to forgive my anxiety and my desire to control the situation. I asked forgiveness for my upset feelings about HIS timing in not letting this happen during the summer. That was MY plan and obviously not HIS."

Sandy describes their hurried trip: "The devil tried really hard to make trouble on our journey...terrible traffic for that time of day, a rock was thrown at my windshield, and I had started getting a migraine, but God prevailed and we made it safely. Traffic cleared, the window didn't crack, and my migraine is gone!"

August 17: Finally, Scott was in surgery. His diseased liver was removed and a new, healthy liver was set in its place. Ordinarily, this surgery has a high success rate and usually goes smoothly with the patient recovering nicely and going home within a few weeks to recuperate and resume a normal lifestyle.

But, it was not to be.

Although the liver was transplanted successfully, other things went wrong. With excessive bleeding and tearing of tissue more than 100 units of blood were given to Scott during surgery and everything could not be completed. The next day when they took him to surgery to finish the job, one of the doctors said "He's not out of the woods yet, but we know he's a Christian man and God is working on him."

The day after Scott's second surgery, Sandy writes: "The doctors and nurses are still amazed at how well Scott is doing. His blood work looks great and they said he is doing a lot better at this point than they thought he would be. Prayer request: Because he lost so much blood during surgery and required 175 units of blood product (along with tons of fluid), his kidneys were overwhelmed. They have just put in an additional line to begin a temporary dialysis to jump start his kidneys. They say this is normal and that it shouldn't last more than a few days. Thank you so much for continuing to pray for Scott's recovery. We truly feel blessed to have SO many people praying for us."

August 27: Ten days after Scott's surgery, when he was still having ups and downs, Sandy was in the cafeteria when she saw a young doctor who had worked on Scott's case when Scott was there in May. The doctor stopped her and asked how Scott was doing. Sandy writes: "I was completely shocked that she remembered me, much less our names! Later in the afternoon, she stopped by Scott's room to see him and said that our family's positive attitude and obvious love for each other made such an impression on her that she's often thought of us. We know that she was seeing God through us and that's what "set us apart" from the hundreds of patients she's seen since May. What a great feeling!"

Ups and downs in Scott's recovery continued long after 'downs' should not have been an issue. During the next months, one thing after another cropped up: Endoscopies and procedures for bleeding in the throat, infection and elevated white blood count, fluid in the lungs, continued kidney dialysis, and blood clots. Sandy's emails had such comments as: "Today we've felt like we were on a roller coaster ride" or "The devil didn't like our praises, so he decided to give us a small stumbling block with …."

After one such "down," she wrote: "At first, Scott and I were obviously disappointed and I had to remind myself that God knew this would happen. We both asked forgiveness for our negative attitude and started praising Him for the victories He gave us this morning."

On October 1, 2013, Sandy wrote: "Praises, praises!!! As of right now Scott is considered "medically stable." They will continue to monitor him through this week. IF he remains stable, they will discharge him next week!"

October 2: "It's hard to believe that less than 12 hours ago Scott's doctors were still talking to me about discharging him next week. I think that's what makes today so hard. Through the night, Scott spiked a fever and his heart rate went up. Transplant was notified immediately and a barrage of tests began (blood work, cultures, EKG, chest x-ray, etc). His temperature is down this morning and one of the docs said this *may* not be anything to worry about. I will know more once all the results are in.

"'*For I know the plans I have for you, declares the LORD, plans to prosper you and not to harm you, plans to give you hope and a future. Then you will call on me and come and pray to me, and I will listen to you. You will seek me and find me when you seek me with all your heart.*' Jeremiah 29:11-13. That is my prayer for today - we are seeking God with all our hearts and trusting HIS plan for us. We are believing that He is listening and gives us hope and a future."

A couple days later when the doctor's found a blood clot in a vein between the heart and liver, she wrote: "Although I have prayed a lot today, God has also given me a peace that HE is in control and He will safely guide the doctors. Once again so many doctors, nurses, and hospital staff have stopped by to see how I was doing. Most of them were surprised that I was doing so well today. I just told them that God had given me peace about this. I was reminded of this verse today and have repeated it many times throughout today: '*Being confident of this, that he who began a good work in you will carry it on to completion until the day of Christ Jesus*' Philippians 1:6."

The next week - October 13: When a pocket of fluid was found in Scott's lungs, she wrote: "Yesterday and today have been a little harder on me for some reason. I am doing my best to take care of myself too, but have been missing our girls and our family just being together. I know that this is God's plan for our family and HE is giving me strength each day, but my "mommy-heart" longs to be together as a family. It seems that every time I feel "down," someone will stop by his room or stop me in the hall and ask about Scott. Several have even said they're praying for us. I know that we have made an impact here, but can't wait to go home."

A few days later as she was driving to the hospital, she said: "I started humming. Although I didn't realize I was humming until I was in the parking garage (I guess the echo of my hum kinda startled me). After I saw Scott and sat down I began to mouth the words and it dawned on me what song it was. *'Surely the Presence of the Lord is in this Place.'* I haven't heard that song in years! I'm surprised I remembered most of the words. As I pray that for this very room, that is also my prayer for each of you -- I pray that you feel the presence of the Lord today."

October 22, 2013: After surgery on Scott's lung (with much bleeding), he was given a tracheotomy to replace the ventilator that had been helping him breath. It was a day Sandy described as "emotionally draining."

Here's what she wrote: "The devil has thrown several things my way today (here and back home), but I know that God is stronger and I keep reminding myself that NONE of this is a surprise to Him. Last night I read one of God's promises - *Deuteronomy 20:1 - 'When you go to war against your enemies and see horses and chariots and an army greater than yours, do not be afraid of them, because the LORD your God, who brought you up out of Egypt, will be with you.'* God promised He would be with the Israelites and help them fight - even when they were outnumbered. Today I've been claiming this promise and fully believe that He IS with me and He WILL help me face whatever comes next. That is definitely a comfort. *"But He knows the way that I take; When He has tested me, I shall come forth as gold." Job 23:10.* Scott and I believe God is allowing us to be tested for a reason, for HIS purpose. We may never know why, we just have to trust in His plan."

On November 25, over three months after his transplant surgery, Scott was helped out of his bed and into a wheelchair. In Sandy's words, it was a "monumental event." Although it was a real struggle, Scott himself pushed the wheels on the chair around the unit, while nurses cheered him on, saying, "Go, Scott!"

Sandy wrote: "I just watched and cried. As we were going through the doorway, I sent a text to our Transplant Nurse Practitioner saying, "If you're not busy, come to the hallway near the elevator." I guess she thought something was wrong, because she came running (literally). When she saw Scott sitting in the wheelchair by the windows, she gasped and started crying with me. Then one of his surgeons came over to see him and said, "Seeing this is one of the great things about my job." It took about 45 minutes for this 'adventure,' but he did it! *'This is the day which the Lord hath made, we will rejoice and be glad in it.'"*

By the middle of December, the therapist had Scott walking while holding to parallel bars with support. One of his surgeons saw him walking and talked about the improvement he'd seen since he saw Scott two weeks earlier. Sandy wrote: "He commented on how hard Scott has been fighting to get better..., saying 'I don't know of anyone else who could go through everything you've been through, and still be here. You must have a lot to live for.' At that point, Scott didn't have his speaking valve on his trach; so Scott just smiled, nodded his head toward me and pointed his finger toward God. HE is what we're living for! *Yet I will rejoice in the LORD, I will joy in the God of my salvation'* Habakkuk 3:18."

Christmas 2013: "The last few days have been pretty busy (in a good way). Scott was at the hospital and doing fairly well and I was able to spend a few days at home with the girls. After waking up at home Christmas morning, we drove to the hospital to be with Scott. The girls were so excited to spend time with Daddy again, he was thrilled to see them and I was happy to have our family in one place. His parents also came up later and we were all able to be together! We definitely long for the day when we can all be together for good!

"Because Scott's white blood count is still bouncing around and they want to see how his new antibiotic is working, the doctors have told me they would not consider moving him to rehab until after the first of the year. I was a bit disappointed at first, but the docs assured me that moving after the holidays would probably be best for him anyway. We will move when it's God's time."

A few days after Christmas, Sandy wrote: "Before Christmas I saw a patient's family member several times in the ICU hallway. We exchanged an occasional "Hi" or head nod. Today I saw her in the cafeteria. She said, "You're still here? My dad has been moved to the floor, but I wondered about you. You're always smiling. Are you still in the ICU?"

"I said yes and asked about her Christmas. She proceeded to tell me how difficult Christmas was this year and how tired she was after being here at the hospital for nine days. I just stood there, listened, and told her I'd pray for her dad's recovery. Then she started asking me about my loved one and if he'd be home by New Year's Day. I told her a little about Scott and casually mentioned that we'd been here for 19 weeks. She was shocked and then apologized for complaining about being there nine days.

"I told her I don't think God has given us a *bigger* burden than anyone else - just a *different* burden. I said her dad being here for nine days was just as big to her, as our journey is to us. She said, "You're a Christian aren't you? I can tell your faith is what's keeping you going right now."

"I was thankful that a perfect stranger noticed Jesus in me. Although I was surprised at first, I shouldn't be surprised that HE answered my prayer - I've been praying I can stay strong and people here would see Jesus in me. *'Surely God is my salvation; I will trust and not be afraid. The LORD, the LORD himself is my strength and my defense; he has become my salvation' Isaiah 12:2.*"

In January, 2014, after 23 weeks in ICU, Scott was transferred to the Transitional Care Hospital (the Rehab center). ICU nurses and doctors lined up to wave and cheer him on.

Less than ten hours later, he was back in ICU. Sandy wrote: "I'll be honest and admit that I was very upset, cried all the way to the hospital, and just didn't understand why God was allowing this. This morning I had to remind myself and two upset little girls, that God knew this was going to happen - it was not a surprise to Him. Since there was no real medical crisis; we are choosing to look at this as a change of plans instead of a setback. God is faithful! *'Wait on the LORD; be of good courage, and he shall strengthen your heart; Wait, I say, on the LORD' Psalm 56:4.*"

By March, Scott was still on a regular dialysis schedule for his kidneys, still had recurring infection because his bone marrow did not make enough blood platelets, still had pockets of fluid pop up now and then in his chest, and was still on a ventilator at night. On the positive side, he was able to take steps with a walker and eat some food to supplement his tube feeding.

In the middle of March, Sandy wrote: "On my drive to the hospital, I was thinking about what may and may not happen and when. I realized.....where we were - God was, where we are - God is, and where we're going - God will be there too! He will not leave us, what a comforting feeling."

On April 19, Sandy shared happy news about Paige's birthday: "The girls and I went home for a few days during the middle of the week and came back to the hospital on Friday. It was Paige's 13th birthday (yes, I'm still in shock that we now have a teenager) and Scott had made sure everyone knew it. During Physical/Occupational Therapy this week, they had Scott make a bracelet and earrings for Paige (I cried when he gave them to her). Several doctors, nurses, and staff stopped by just to tell her Happy Birthday. Earlier in the week, the Transplant Team had asked what kind of cake she liked and after we had been there about an hour, some of the Team walked into Scott's room with a cake, card, and balloons - WOW - I felt blessed by the number of people here that took time to help make her birthday special."

In May, 2014, there were still ups and downs, but the good news was, "Scott continues to progress with Physical Therapy. Last week he walked farther than he has before and even climbed 13 stairs with help - go Scott!!. On Friday, the trach was removed and he's breathing great - YAY! Right now, the plans are to send him home soon (maybe even this upcoming week)."

The hope was that Scott would be discharged from the hospital **on June 7,** ten months after what should have been no more than a few week hospital stay. Instead, he spiked a fever, had to have blood transfusions and developed a fluid pocket in his abdomen.

One week later, Sandy's phone rang at 4:30am with news that Scott had apparently sleep walked. In his weak condition, he fell, causing a small fracture in his upper left arm and another on the left side of his pelvis, along with a bad gash on his head and a slight concussion.

Sandy wrote: "As word spread, people started coming up to his room to check on him. Several doctors and nurses even hugged me and said they were sorry this happened when he was doing so well. Although I was emotional throughout the day, I just reminded them that God still protected Scott during the fall. There were times today, when I just wanted to ask God how much more could Scott's body handle. For now, I'll just keep trusting that Scott is truly in HIS hands and no matter what the doctors' say or do...GOD is in control. *'....I am he, I am he who will sustain you. I have made you and I will carry you; I will sustain you and I will rescue you'* Isaiah 46:4."

The end of June, Sandy wrote, "After a bleeding 'incident' last Monday, a doc said to me 'You know Sandy, I was watching you help out, then I was looking at Scott and I said to myself, This is true love! I was upset about my broken engagement, but she did not love me the way you love him. That's what I want.' I simply can't imagine not doing what I've been doing for Scott. I don't understand this path, but accept it as God's plan."

August 17, 2014: The one year anniversary of Scott's liver transplant, Sandy shared her feelings: "Today is a day of THANKS that needs to be recognized," and she proceeded to thank God for Scott's new liver and the family who donated such a gift in the midst of their own grief; for safety in traveling back and forth, for the wonderful doctors, nurses and techs, and for friends and family who pray and have been such great support.

"Because there have been many steps forward as well as backward, Scott is still in the hospital. Yes, this means he's been there a full year today...but...he is still here, and for that I am THANKFUL! It's been a difficult year with many sinking lows and even some incredible highs, but all in all we honestly have so much to be thankful for.

"**In the last 365 days...** I've learned more medical 'stuff' than I ever thought my little brain could handle, I've made so many new friends, cried (a lot), laughed (laughter is the best medicine, right?), eaten more brownies than I should have, and realized just how THANKFUL I should have been before. God has taught me so much this year. Now, I always look at a situation and find something to be THANKFUL for. I encourage you to find something to be thankful for today."

Sept 13, Sandy wrote, "By Friday, the Transplant Team decided they were ready for him to go to the floor. When I got here yesterday afternoon, he had already moved. The nurse told me they let Scott WALK to his new room (using the walker, of course) and they rolled his bed behind him. One nurse said, there were several people just cheering him on (that made me smile). We've had a good day together today. I wheeled him out to the atrium and we were able to spend about an hour out there. Scott didn't want to come back inside yet, but I was afraid his nurse would think I had loaded him in my car and headed home. ;-)"

Sept 24: "I was a little discouraged this morning when I got the nurse's text saying Scott's blood platelets had dropped drastically overnight, but felt better this afternoon when she assured me that overall Scott was doing okay. I'm taking comfort knowing that God has called Scott by name - He knows the number of platelets Scott needs."

Nov. 3: "After an up and down week, last week ended on a good note. Paige and I were able to go see Scott early on Friday, while Sidney came with Scott's parents came later that afternoon. On Saturday, we celebrated Scott's birthday!! The girls decorated his room with streamers, and I set up a 'beach party' outside his room for the doctors, nurses, and staff. It was nice to see so many people stop by his room to wish him a Happy Birthday.

    The girls have been praying that Daddy will be home by Thanksgiving. Although all things are possible with God, I'm not sure this is feasible, I pray they are not too disappointed (yet again) if God has other plans for Scott."

Nov. 22: Scott had a really good week until this morning, he spiked a fever and was having difficulty breathing. The CT Scan showed a small amount of pneumonia. Thankfully, he's feeling better, but extremely disappointed that this means he will not be home for Thanksgiving. I was in tears most of Saturday morning. I know God has a plan, but I just wasn't looking forward to telling the girls we'd be celebrating Thanksgiving at the hospital again (they have been fervently praying he'd be home by then).

Nov. 26: "Just a quick note to let you know Scott's surgeon decided he needed to be home for Thanksgiving. I just wanted you all to know that I brought Scott HOME late tonight and our little family is all together. Only God could do this! Please continue to pray for Scott's healing (we still have a long way to go). *'In everything give thanks; for this is the will of God in Christ Jesus concerning you I Thessalonians 5:18.'*"

Nov. 30: "While these last four days have been busy, it's been great having Scott home. This morning, Scott was having trouble breathing and his temp was a little higher than it should be. After speaking with his nurse and spending three hours in the local ER, the Transplant Team decided they needed to see Scott, so the university hospital flight team ended up coming to get him and flying him to the hospital. Scott was not really thrilled about having to go back to the hospital, but they did warn us this would happen."

Wednesday, Dec. 10: Scott's last time at home ended after three sleepless nights and a trip back to the hospital, but Sandy had not given up hope. She wrote, "I fully believe that God has something big planned for our family, I'm just waiting to see what He does. When we left the hospital last Sunday, a nurse texted me that evening saying she was happy we were home again, she'd miss us, and then she said I was "an example of perseverance and limitless faith." I've never thought of myself like that. *'Now faith is the substance of things hoped for, the evidence of things not seen' Hebrews 11:1."*

Dec. 28, 2014: "Scott wanted the girls to wake up at home Christmas morning. Afterwards, we drove to the hospital to be with him for a few days. Not only did I get the two things I asked for this year (a new hair dryer and-my little family to be together) and the girls got most of the things on their list...but we were blessed more than we could have ever imagined!

First of all, we were blessed to be with Scott and that he was having a good day. He even enjoyed opening the presents we brought him (Star Wars ornaments and movies, of course!). Next, so many of you allowed God to use you to bless our family (with gifts, notes of encouragement, meals, and most importantly - prayers). Then, several people at the hospital brought little things to my girls, told me how impressed they were with them, and how our family had so much faith that they could see we were different - wow, what a gift. I want others to see Him in us! In a small way, I felt that we were able to give God a gift too!"

Jan. 3, 2015 "The year started much differently than we had hoped. We were hoping to be together at home, but that was not what God had planned for us. We are thankful we could be together though!"

Feb. 8: "For some time now, I've been dealing with the reality that our life will never be "normal" again (in that we won't have the same life we had before Scott got sick). We prayed for a new liver and thought that would 'fix' everything. Little did we know all this other stuff would happen and Scott would still be in the hospital 18 months later. I continually remind myself that none of this was a surprise to God - it's been His plan all along!! It doesn't mean I have to like it, but I do have to accept it as His will for our lives. We do realize that God is using us and we will continue to give Him the glory in ALL things."

Feb. 16: "Our girls (Paige more than Sidney) have asked some difficult questions lately. Please pray for their peace and that I will have the right words as I answer their questions. It's hard when I don't know the answers or understand myself why God has placed this path before us.

We just have to trust that He does have a plan, even when we can't see it. *'So we fix our eyes not on what is seen, but on what is unseen, since what is seen is temporary, but what is unseen is eternal' 2 Corinthians 4:18."*

March 29: "There's a lot to the story, but I'm going to try to briefly give some facts. Months ago, we were told that Scott's pneumonia had become resistant to almost every antibiotic they've used....they only had one left. As of Friday, he has built up a resistance to that one too and it's no longer working. Because there is no other way to treat this pneumonia and the other "issues" he's having, the collective decision has been to make Scott as comfortable as possible. This has been a long journey and it's hard to believe that THIS is how God would end it, but we're choosing to believe that He has a plan and is still in complete control of Scott's life (and ours).

For now, the girls are spending as much time as they can with their Daddy! I have had some of the toughest conversations of my life over the last three days. Please be in prayer for them. Scott's biggest desire is to come home to be a dad again and in my opinion, this is the hardest part.

The doctors and nurses have been very compassionate and most have been very emotional as they talk to us. So many people (docs, nurses, techs, staff - tons of people) have stopped by to talk to either Scott or me and some have expressed how sorry they are. I try to tell them that I agree it's not fair that Scott has fought so hard and isn't winning the fight, *but* because we believe and we have faith...this is not the end, we **WILL** see Scott again.

We are not ruling out a miracle, but that's what it would take at this point. Thank you all for traveling this journey with us. *'My flesh and my heart may fail, but God is the strength of my heart and my portion forever' Psalm 73:26."*

March 31: "Right now, we are just enjoying being together as a family. I have read many of your messages to Scott when he was awake. Some of them he made comments on, others made him smile (he has an awesome smile). Thanks again for bombarding God with prayers for our family! *'I will praise you as long as I live, and in your name I will lift up my hands' Psalm 63:4."*

April 2, 2015: "Some of you already know, but my sweet husband is now breathing with both lungs fully inflated and the other *issues* his body was having have now been healed! Please continue to pray for our girls. I was an adult when my Dad passed away, I can't imagine losing him at a young age. It has been such an emotional few days, but the outpouring of love and support at the hospital has been absolutely amazing. *'For this God is our God for ever and ever; he will be our guide even to the end' Psalm 48:14.*"

June 21, 2015 – Father's Day: "For Father's Day today, the girls and I did several things to remember and honor Scott. We continued our tradition of having Krispy Kreme donuts for breakfast, had lunch with some special friends whose Dad is overseas serving our country in the Navy, went to the beach and walked on the boardwalk (Father's Day was always spent at the beach), and had Daddy's favorite pizza and ice cream for dinner.

There were definitely difficult and tear-filled moments today. Especially this morning -- maybe because the girls used to always wake Daddy up on Father's Day with lots of love, kisses, and homemade cards. We talked about it and reminded ourselves that Daddy is getting to spend Father's Day with our Heavenly Father and that even though we miss him greatly, he had a wonderful Father's Day! I'm thankful for all the prayers today - we felt them!

'So that your trust may be in the LORD; I teach you today, even you' Proverbs 22:19. Today, God taught me that I can make it through a holiday like Father's Day, even when I didn't think I could."

He heals the brokenhearted and binds up their wounds.
Psalm 147:3

-Photo: This courtesy photo of Sandy and her precious family was taken at the hospital just before they left for Scott's first visit home

CINDY

When Cindy began attending our Bible study a few years ago, I was impressed with her self-confidence and spiritual maturity. Not only that, she is also an attractive woman with a ready smile, sense of humor and friendly spirit. Having observed these things in Cindy, I was surprised to hear that she has a myriad of health problems and had struggled with deep guilt for most of her life. She said, "Much of my life, I believed that the essence of me was bad. That all I did was cause pain and destruction."

Cindy Shares her Story:

"I was the second of five children. When I was born a month early, the doctor took one look at me and said, "We never should have let this baby live." Not a particularly auspicious entry into the world, but that was just the beginning.

The first indication something was wrong happened every time my mom patted my back to burp me. Each time, I screamed in pain. My parents took me from one doctor to another with no results. When I was eight months old, Mom noticed I was dragging my legs instead of crawling. They operated on my spine and found a tumor the length of the spinal cord with bits and pieces of hair and fingernails indicating I was probably a twin who had been joined in the spine. They could not remove the tumor because it was entangled in the spinal cord and removal would have caused severe nerve damage. They closed me up and told my parents I had a 50/50 chance to live and if I did live I would be paralyzed from the waist down and never walk.

This devastating news led my mother to the church. She was desperate to find the strength to live with such a horrible diagnosis. Two weeks later my father gave his life to the Lord. My parents became strong believers, and we went to church every Sunday. It's amazing to me how the Lord uses tragedy to get our attention and ultimately bring us to Him.

Despite the doctor's grim prognosis, I did live and at the age of three, I began to walk -- a double miracle. However, I was left internally paralyzed.

Throughout my early childhood, I had major problems with my bladder, kidneys and bowels and I had to wear diapers. My feet became clubbed and the arch in one foot was so high I could touch my toes to my heel. My life became one surgery after another. They did five surgeries when I was six years old just trying to construct a new bladder.

Imagine starting school at the age of six and carrying a diaper bag to class every day. At the time, it was normal for me, but when my best friend took my diaper bag and threw it into the hallway at school for all to see, I experienced for the first time that I was different and not accepted by the other kids because of that. When I relive that horrifying, humiliating moment, my heart is saddened for the hurting little girl that I was.

At the age of eight, I'd already flunked first grade for missing so much school, and instead of wearing diapers I was now wearing an ostomy bag. I continued to be made fun of – now it was for having a bag.

When I was ten years old, my mom had a complete nervous breakdown and stayed in the hospital over a month. When she came home she was heavily medicated and very fragile. We five kids didn't know which mom we were going to come home from school and find -- the happy mom or the angry, agitated mom. We were told that we better be good or our behavior would put her in a mental hospital, and we would never see her again. We learned at an early age that we were responsible for the emotional state of other people.

I will never forget the day my mother told my brother and I that we were responsible for her breakdown because of all my medical problems and his emotional issues. He had brain damage from birth, causing a split personality which started around four years old.

That message from her, and having to deal with being physically different from everyone else motivated me to rebel. By the time I was in junior high, I was stealing, smoking, cussing and skipping school. I was one messed up kid.

When I was 12 years old, I had my first foot operation. That's when I became addicted to pain medication. In order to straighten my foot, they had to break the major bones in the foot. They also cut the arch in the other foot to lower it. As if that was not painful and debilitating enough, they broke all the toes in both feet and put a pin in each to keep them straight during the healing. I was in the hospital for a month and getting pain medication every four hours. I came home from the hospital in a wheel chair with both feet in a cast.

Because of complications, I was soon back in the hospital where I remained for months. It became my home. They fed me through a tube in my nose. I loved all the nurses because they were kind to me; I didn't have to do any chores and most of all I didn't have to deal with mom.

After a few months, I had to go back to my real home and I was miserable. It wasn't long before I was taking medication from mom's medicine cabinet and hooking up with kids who introduced me to marijuana and hash. At the age of 13, I was on the road to self-destruct. I wanted to do more and more drugs – enough so that I would never feel pain again.

I remember looking at myself in the mirror one day and thinking, 'What man will ever want me?' I had an ostomy bag, was told I could never have children; and had scars and missing toes. I felt like I was a reject that had somehow gotten off the assembly line and made it to earth. I wondered what kind of God would have done this to a person. Why would a loving God make me with all these problems? I cursed Him and said, 'The hell with you.'

One day when I was about 14 years old, I asked mom if I could go out to be with my boyfriend. When she said no, I told her we were a lot happier when she was in the hospital. Shortly afterward, I walked by her bedroom and saw her crying and writing something on a piece of paper. The next thing I know, my dad intercepted her in the driveway with a loaded gun in her purse. She'd planned on driving to a dead end road and killing herself.

Mom was taken to the hospital for another mental breakdown. This time I believed it actually was my fault. I remember running outside, hiding in the azalea bushes, crying and believing that I had almost killed my mother. The enemy was right there accusing me and making me feel responsible for my mother's near suicide. Here was another accusation confirming the fact that I never should have been born. Not only was I a mistake, but I was now responsible for almost killing our mother. What a terrible, horrible person I was!

When I was fifteen years old, my life changed. That was when I ended up getting busted for having drugs in my room. My parents called the police (who did a good job of scaring me!), and then decided to put me in a Christian school to get me away from corrupt friends. I was grounded and not allowed to go anywhere with my friends.

To this day I do not know how I passed the entrance exam to get into the Christian school. It was certainly of God. Going to Christian school was like going to a different country for me. I was the only one in the school who cussed or smoked. I got caught smoking the first day. I hated it.

One day, another student invited me to go with her to a Bible Study she was attending. I wasn't interested in the Bible study, but I thought at least I could get out of the house and smoke and hang out with some kids. I asked mom and dad, and they gave me permission to go.

The woman teaching the lesson began to explain how God loved us so much that He sent His son to earth to die on the cross for our sins. As she explained the gospel, I began asking her questions. I went home not really understanding, but it was definitely scratching an itch I didn't even know I had.

The next week I went back mainly because I was still on restriction. That week the teacher talked about Psalm 139 and how God knit you together in your mother's womb and that you weren't a mistake. She said that everyone has something they don't like about themselves. I thought to myself, you aren't kidding!

That night I went into my room and stood by my bed. I said, 'God, I am going nowhere with my life. I am on the road to self-destruction and if it's true that you loved me enough to die for me and take away my sins, then I give you my life.' In that moment I felt this warm light come into the room and I heard a voice say, 'Anyone can be normal, but I have made you different because you are special.'

Something changed in me that night. I was not the same person. God had dealt with the two main issues in my life -- my guilt at almost killing my mother, and my feelings of being a reject on the assembly line of humanity. How amazing is He!

I was a transformed person. I soon quit smoking and began playing the guitar and singing. I began sharing the good news with my old friends, most of whom promptly disowned me as their friend. I became chaplain of my junior class. My life turned around that night. I no longer looked at myself as a mistake but as someone special that God had created for His unique and special purpose.

In spite of the fact that I'd experienced a dramatic life changing conversion, there were still heart issues that needed to be dealt with. It wasn't until marriage that I began to be aware of those areas in my heart that were bound up and in need of attention.

I met Gary at a Christian Retreat in 1973 when I was nineteen years old. I attended the retreat with my boyfriend (whom I'd just agreed to marry). Gary led the songs and he was in charge of the games. I'd just graduated from high school – the same school where Gary taught history and Bible.

Everything was fine between my boyfriend and I until Gary stood up and started leading the games. Oh my goodness, from that moment on I could not even remember the name of the young man that I had just days ago agreed to marry. The only name on my mind was Gary! I found myself wanting to be with him and listen to him express his views on Biblical issues. He was out of the box concerning the main line conservative views that I'd been taught in my Christian school and I found it all very intriguing. He seemed to be the missing link that helped me understand about some of those teachings I just hadn't been able to go along with. And – let's be honest! It didn't hurt that he was very handsome and a dashing six years older than me. OK, I was smitten!

Gary had been a Christian since he was eleven years old and began leading the youth group in his church at the age of fourteen. I felt I could trust him to lead me as a husband. His beliefs were in line with mine and we appeared to be equally yoked as far as we could tell.

I also knew that his home life was a mess. His father was emotionally abusive – a man full of anger and rage fueled by self-pity. This same man took his family to Church every Sunday, sang in the choir, laughed with his friends and behaved like any normal Christian man, but as soon as the family was in the car and the door shut, the mean angry father reappeared, telling everyone what a disappointment they were. As a result, Gary's mother became withdrawn. All this meant that he had feelings of being emotionally abandoned and unloved by both parents.

Even though I was saved, my perception of God was distorted. Part of me believed what God's word said and another part of me couldn't. A part of my mind was stuck believing that I was too bad to come before God. I believed that all I did was cause pain and destruction.

These were the backgrounds Gary and I came from – each of us with deep emotional misconceptions and needs that had never been addressed. These were the toxic undercurrents with which we began our marriage.

Every time my husband said something negative about what I did all I could hear in my head was, 'You are bad, you never should have been able to live. You are bad.' I became defensive in my response, saying, "Well, I didn't mean to do it," or "it wasn't my fault," or "That's not what I meant" -- anything that would deflect what I felt was an incoming missile that confirmed the belief that "I was bad." Or sometimes, I just shut down and didn't communicate which my husband took as meaning that I must not love him.

On the other hand, Gary believed that his wife was going to compensate for all the love he didn't get as a child. So when I said something that questioned my love for him he would become either angry and dispute why that wasn't true, or become depressed and just lay around feeling sad that he was not loved. It became a vicious cycle.

What was really going on in us? My responses to Gary exposed his belief that he was not good enough to be loved. Likewise, I realized shortly into our marriage that I had married my mother. I could not fix her as a child, so I married her. Hoping that if I could fix Gary, I would bring value to myself instead of believing that, "After all, If Cindy had not been born with all her medical problems, then mom would not have had her breakdowns and the family would have been better off.'

By our 15th year of marriage Gary had been to seminary, believing God was calling him to the pastorate. We had our miracle baby girl who was so precious to both of us. We spent five wonderful years in Pennsylvania pastoring a church and seeing many come to Christ through our ministry.

It became necessary for us to leave the church and move back to our hometown to be close to my doctors. For years, I was in and out of hospitals and almost died in 1983 because of infection. Even so, we saw miracle after miracle.

God was real, but we just couldn't get a grip on the issues in our marriage. We had faith, we knew the Word of God and we would pray and ask for wisdom. As this continued, I began to see Gary's anger affecting our daughter. She was becoming afraid of her own father. She woke up at night hearing him yelling at me and she would begin to cry for fear that he was going to hurt me. His anger became more and more explosive and I too became afraid.

The turning point came when I found Jenny with her suitcase packed, planning on running away to my parent's house. I realized how much she was being affected by all this. I had been willing to stick it out, but I knew she needed safety and stability.

We'd gone through some counseling in our fifteen years of marriage, but it had not offered us what we needed and never really addressed our issues. We didn't believe there was any hope for us to get back together.

I moved in with my parents and filed for divorce. I was done trying to make our marriage work. I wanted emotional stability for my daughter and myself -- no more ups and downs. My father built a garage and a second-floor apartment for Jenny and me to live. I was happy living in a safe place.

For a while, Gary thought his life in ministry was over. Then, the Lord spoke to him. He prayed and surrendered, saying, 'Lord if my wife never loves me, if my daughter never loves me, if I can only hand out bulletins at Church -- Lord your love is enough.' Soon after, he felt like he was being called to China and he went.

This gave Jenny and me a time of peace so that we could begin the healing process. The Lord knew exactly what we needed. I worked with my mom at her boutique. I loved working with the women who came in. I became good at accessorizing the customers with jewelry and belts and scarves. I learned how to dress the windows, and mom took me to market with her to pick out clothes for the next season.

I was thankful for this time to be with my mom and the healing God gave me. She herself had received major healing from the Lord for her mental condition. You would never have known she was the same woman. Those were good times and we were thankful for God's goodness.

Gary got a job teaching English in China. He was also busy transporting Bibles all over China. In the process he got to know many leaders of the house churches. A major revival was going on there, and he loved being in the middle of God's action. During this time, the Lord told Gary that He wanted him to return home to be with Jenny while she was going to high school because she needed her father.

Jenny and I had been living above my parent's garage almost four years. I'd been suffering from a chronic condition for a long time, but now it had become severe and I was losing weight, dropping down to 89 pounds. As my physical problem worsened, I found a surgeon who agreed to operate. The date was set, and suddenly I began to panic. What if I die? Who is going to take care of Jenny? I could imagine Gary coming back and taking her to China, getting arrested and her being put in prison with him. I was full of fear thinking I might die, and worrying about my daughter!

That weekend, Jenny went on a retreat with the youth group. Meanwhile, I was home wondering and worrying about the 'What if?' Finally I heard the Lord break in with the question, 'Don't you know that I love Jenny even more than you love her?' I said yes. 'And don't you know that your life is in my hands?' I said, Yes, I know.

Then God said, 'Will you give me Jenny?' With tears and a bit of hesitation I gave Him the most precious thing I had. She was the love of my life -- my reason for living. I saw her in my hands as I raised them and placed her into His hands.

When I went to pick Jenny up after the retreat, I told her about my meeting with God and my surrender. She looked at me and said, 'Mom, I was sharing with the group that you were going to have surgery and might die. I began to cry and one of my friends came over to me and asked me if I had given my mom to the Lord? With tears, I gave you to the Lord, Mom.'

We both sat there in the car and cried in each other's arms -- amazed at God's grace.

In August 1993, Gary returned to the U.S. When he landed, he had no job, no place to live, and no car. The Lord had told him to return home and he had -- with nothing but two suit cases. The first miracle happened when God supplied an apartment – free of charge. The next day he was given a car. Then God gave him a job with a ministry starting a work in China. To top off this series of miracles, the man had office space at a major Christian Ministry that was in the same city and state where we were living.

February 23, 1994, I was singing in the Choir at church. As we sang about walls coming down I suddenly felt the Lord moving in my heart. I felt like Moses standing before the Red Sea and God was stirring the waters, I heard Him say, 'Watch and see what I am going to do!' I did not think about Gary in that moment. I had no idea what the Lord meant, but I felt anticipation stir up within me.

Apparently the Lord moved in Gary's heart that morning too. He asked the Lord what he wanted him to do and he felt the Lord say, 'Buy a car.' Gary had been looking at a few different cars to buy so he went out and bought the one that made the most sense. Afterward he thought -- what now Lord? He didn't get an answer, so he thought, I'll go and show Jenny the car!

Gary drove the new-used car to my house to show it to Jenny. When I told him Jenny wasn't there, he asked if I'd like to take a spin with him. I agreed and as we talked, I felt that something was very different. When we got back home and sat in the car talking, I realized the wall was down. There was no barrier between us. I invited him inside and within a short period of time we knew God was putting us back together. We were in shock but we both knew the Lord was doing it.

The next morning, I told my mom, 'I don't understand what is happening but I do believe the Lord is bringing Gary and I back together.' I will never forget the look on her face. A big smile appeared and she began telling me that eight months ago she and dad were discussing my situation of being alone and wondering what was going to happen. They went to bed and the Lord woke her up and told her not to worry about Cindy, that He had saved her for her husband and He would bring them back together.

We were-married June 5, 1994 in the Mennonite Church that had sent Gary off to China. Our wedding was held during the Sunday morning service with much singing and rejoicing for the amazing work God had done in all our lives. Jenny sang and my dad officiated at the wedding. We had our reception at Mom and Dad's. It was our second wedding, but it was our best wedding.

For me, the journey to find healing has happened when I've been willing to connect with the little Cindy that went through traumatic events in her childhood; who heard messages that were not truth-based, but were lie-based. The lie was that Cindy should never have been born -- everybody would have been better off without her.

What an awesome reward we get in allowing the Lord to take us through the process of receiving healing with a knowledge of Him that comes only by going through the trenches, facing our enemy and finding our Lord and Savior who is in the trenches with us leading us on into victory.

The truth is that God ordained my birth and my life. In fact, He used me to bring my parents to Him and many others as well. He has used me to motivate healing for my husband by exposing some of his own lie-based thinking. The truth is that I have a Heavenly Father who loves me and delights in me coming to Him as a little girl who doesn't have to perform for Him. He can be quite playful with His children."

"You will know the truth, and the truth will set you free"
John 8:32

-Photo: Courtesy photo of Cindy and Gary during the prayer at their second wedding

SHANNON

Shannon and Dave were high school sweethearts – in the same class, at the same Christian school. Four years after they graduated they were married, and a year later they were ready to begin a family. Shannon said, "I always wanted to get married and be a Mom. Being a mother was my number one desire."

When their second wedding anniversary came and went with no pregnancy, they shrugged it off, confident it would happen soon. They were busy with jobs – she as a nanny for twins, and he as the manager in a family-owned business. They both came from supportive Christian homes and their families were encouraging, telling them they were young and had plenty of time to start a family. It would happen in God's time.

Shannon shares how she felt as the third and fourth anniversary rolled around, and still no baby on the horizon: "I felt like something was wrong with me as a woman. I went through not wanting to go to baby showers and not talking to anyone about it, to being obsessed with my need for a baby."

Shannon was saved at the age of seven years old. Dave was brought up in a Christian family and now says he realizes he had what might be called, "an inherited faith" that comes from knowing all about Jesus, but not making a personal decision of salvation. He was saved in 2006 during his darkest hour.

They both grew up in Sunday School and Christian School and they'd heard all the Bible stories about Hannah and Sarah's quest for babies, and God's answering blessings. They knew God was in control, but as Shannon says, " When it's happening to you, it's easy to lose perspective – even become frantic. We just wanted a child."

After years with no results, the couple decided to try in vitro fertilization process in hopes of getting that longed-for baby. They went through seven rounds of in vitro – a grueling, painful, expensive process – with no success and only dashed hopes -- they were frustrated and depressed.

"Dave was ready to adopt way before I was. I kept saying, one more time, one more time."

They refinanced their home and later obtained a second mortgage in order to pay for the expensive medical procedures.

In 2004, they gave up on in vitro treatments and decided they would adopt. "After the seventh round of in vitro, the doctor called and said it was negative. That was our answer from God that we were meant to adopt. I prayed for a clear answer and He gave it to us. We were ready to start the adoption process."

That same year, Dave was involved in an ATV accident and sustained internal bruising injuries. When he was given Percocet for the pain, there was a surprising side effect to the drug – all the depression and feelings of failure he'd been suffering over the years were magically lifted. He felt good – and he liked that feeling so much that when the pain pills ran out, he was desperate to find something to lift the perpetual sadness that clouded his heart and mind.

A friend gave him some OxyContin (with friends like that – who needs enemies?) and it did an even better job of lifting his spirits than the previous pain killers. He said, "It gave me a completely different feeling like I'd never had before. It was a feeling I knew I wanted to feel again." Dave was hooked and that's when his downward spiral began in earnest – and continued for over two years. He began stealing money from his father's business where he worked -- and he became a different person.

Shannon remembers when she discovered his hidden pills, "My heart dropped. I remember thinking, I didn't marry a drug addict. I was so angry. I found the pills on Palm Sunday 2006 before a family dinner. I looked in his briefcase. There was a little tin box and the pills were in it. My mom drove me to a pharmacy. I showed the pharmacist a pill and asked what it was. She said it was OxyContin. When I got back, David was gone. He knew what I'd found and he'd gone to his dad's house. I thought, I can't believe this is happening. I felt like I was going to lose everything. I thought, what has he done?"

On Friday, Dave was taken to a drug detox and rehab facility. Shannon said, "He was screaming, kicking – it was horrible." He stayed in the facility for the weekend and then continued to get help to overcome his addiction. The next month, he returned home.

Shannon said, "I told him, you are getting clean before you come back to the house. He was sorry, crying, asking forgiveness."

It was a dark time for this young couple. They'd been married nine years, sharing good times and hard times, but this was surely the lowest point in their lives.

Then – there was God. When we reach the bottom and there's no place to look but up, God is always there waiting for His children. The day Dave went into rehab, Shannon was praying for a miracle to happen to her husband. At the same time, Dave was crying out to God for that same miracle. God answered their prayers and almost immediately healed Dave of his drug addiction.

When Dave returned home – with God's help -- they began rebuilding their life together. After all this, there was still no child in their home. They had previously applied to adopt a baby from China and were approved the next year.

A year after what Shannon calls, "The drug stuff," Dave began a Christian training process, was ordained and began working in the youth and music ministry of their church in the fall of 2007. Shannon says, "I got pregnant four months later."

She said, "We were taking a youth group to Winter Jam over the weekend. My hormones were crazy. I was crying about a sign I saw picturing babies in China. We had no idea I was pregnant. We were busy going and doing that Monday. I was crying over the slightest thing and snapping at David.

I decided to buy a pregnancy test. When I took the test, I couldn't bring myself to look at the result. When David got home and I told him, he immediately looked at the test. It was positive. He fell to the ground, and started crying like a baby and praising God. I was crying too. Then, we go and get another test and it was positive. We then went to Patient First and took another test and they said, 'Congratulations, you're having a baby.'

After ten years of trying to get pregnant -- the beginning of miracles occurred and Shannon became pregnant.

Shannon and David were ecstatic over this unexpected and blessed pregnancy.

In the meantime, the baby they'd been anxiously awaiting from China was born on April 21, 2008. They named her *Jinger* and looked forward to bringing her home when all the paperwork and waiting period was completed.

On July 6, 2008, more than three months before her due date, Shannon gave birth to a 2-1/2 pound baby girl. She said "I developed toxemia and preeclampsia and she was born at 26 weeks. I knew she was a miracle baby. When I was in the hospital and they were prepping me for an emergency C-section, my mom was so worried. I told everyone that God is going to take care of this baby. She is going to be fine. I had 100% faith this baby was going to be fine – and she is."

Shannon said, "When she was born, I was overwhelmed with joy, and thanking God that I was able to experience a pregnancy."

Although they had now been blessed with this beautiful baby girl – whom they named *Jenna* – she had to stay in the NICU for 2-1/2 months. With all the "mommy hormones" coursing through her body, this was especially hard for Shannon.

To add to her depression, they'd just heard from China that, because they would now have a baby under one year old in the home, China would not let them adopt a baby at this time. Shannon said, "We were both devastated and angry with God. Why the timing like this? Our baby was in the NICU and now we can't get Jinger. We asked God what was up with this?"

God was about to answer Shannon's question. A hymn written by William Cowper in 1773 begins: "God moves in a mysterious way, His wonders to perform..." And what a joy and blessing to see Him work those supernatural wonders!

When Dave picked Shannon up from the hospital and was wheeling her toward the car, he began sharing news with her she did not want to hear. She said, "We left the hospital, having lost the China adoption, then, I couldn't take my baby Jenna home, and Dave starts telling me about a 15-year old couple who didn't want their baby and they wanted us to adopt her. I told him I didn't want to do this. I was afraid it would fall through and I just couldn't handle taking a baby and then losing it.

David talked me into going to this other hospital. We met the 15-year old birth parents, and we met the baby who had been born on July 11. They'd planned to let a couple in California take her, but then decided they wanted a local couple to have her. We said yes and they said yes. We just switched China adoption papers to a domestic adoption and in less than two weeks, we walked out of the hospital with another baby.

Jolie is so meant to be with us, I couldn't imagine her being anywhere else. God has a perfect plan for everything and He says, 'Shannon, chill out. I'm giving you a baby who is two pounds, then I'm giving you another baby, and when they're six months old, I'm sending you to China to get another baby.'"

Shannon and Dave with Jolie, Jinger & Jenna in 2009

And so, Shannon and David went from being childless to having three daughters – Jinger, Jenna and Jolie -- who are practically the same age. Shannon said, "When we'd take them places in a triple stroller, people would stop and ask, 'Oh, are they triplets?' I would want to point out that one of them is Chinese, but Dave just stopped and joyfully shared the whole miraculous story."

Shannon smiles, "They may not be triplets, but they are sisters – and they're all mine."

Shannon remembers the nice house they used to have – a house they lost in foreclosure as a result of all that happened in their lives. She says, "Would I trade that big, beautiful home we had for what I have with David and my girls in a cracker box house, and my kids being able to go to Christian School? I would much rather choose this. This is where we're supposed to be, and I praise God every time I pull into the driveway."

Shannon smiles as she finishes her story with words of assurance: "We've all gone through trials. We don't always understand why we go through these things, but He has a plan. I know His timing is absolutely perfect and He has a reason for everything. I'm a walking testimony with these children."

One of Shannon's favorite verses is found in Ephesians 3:20: *"Now to Him who is able to do exceedingly abundantly above all that we ask or think, according to the power that works in us, to Him be glory in the church by Christ Jesus to all generations, forever and ever. Amen."*

-Photo: Courtesy picture of the family when the girls were babies.

LYNDA & CHIP

Most of us have heard the term *the new normal* – meaning "a previously unfamiliar situation that has now become standard," or in everyday terms – "when a traumatic situation turns your life upside down and you learn to live with it as your new everyday way of life."

That's what happened to Lynda and Chip – twice.

Although our story is primarily focused on ordinary women who have gone through extraordinary circumstances, Lynda's husband is included in the mix, because her life-changing story is so intertwined with his life-changing story – and also because Chip will be the primary story-teller due to Lynda's loss of memory of a portion of the events that have shaped their lives.

Lynda and Chip were both saved when they were nine years old. Their stories have been intertwined since they met in fifth grade at Blanton Elementary School in Florida.

Blanton 5th grade class – Chip is far left and Lynda is far right

It was not until his junior year in high school, however, that Chip said, "I got up the nerve to ask her to go out with me. We saw the movie *Funny Girl* and I can still remember how wonderful it felt to hold her hand as we walked out of that theater."

"At the end of our first date," Chip remembers, "I knew there was something very special about this girl. Just three weeks later on our third date, I asked her to marry me. At the age of 16, I knew that I wanted to spend the rest of my life with her."

Three years later in 1971, they were married. Along the way, they had a daughter, Jenny; Chip was in the Navy for over 22 years; and Lynda became a school teacher. They were always devoted to one another and have always felt their marriage is very special.

Lynda says, "My husband and I have been one since we were married. Our love has always been strong."

Chip added, "I'm an incurable romantic when it comes to Lynda. After nearly 44 years of marriage, she is still my girlfriend and I'm still her boyfriend. We are best friends and have spent our life dedicated to making each other happy."

It would be their love and devotion to one another and their deep, abiding faith in God that would get them through two devastating events that could have destroyed their lives.

April 23, 2007 was a normal weekday that found Lynda at the private Christian school where she taught four-year old children. Lynda loved combining her creative abilities and her deep love for children in the classroom. It was a win-win for both she and the children.

Chip, a part-time flight instructor, was scheduled to teach ground school that evening. The class was cancelled and they were able to spend the evening together. Everything seemed normal – except for a very strong headache Lynda had which she attributed to sinus problems.

Chip said, "We had an extremely blessed life together. We had raised a wonderful daughter who was now married and they were in the process of adopting our first grandchild, and we had developed a wonderful extended family through our church. Life was good."

On April 24, after Lynda arrived at school, she still had a headache and began to feel as if she might pass out. They arranged for a substitute teacher and Chip picked her up and took her to the doctor. During the examination, Lynda developed a strange look on her face and started to speak incoherently. This lasted about a minute and then she slowly became oriented, but still had some confusion.

The doctor gave Lynda pain pills and ordered a CAT scan for later that night.

Lynda's confusion continued throughout the evening and she experienced a number of "spells" where she became dizzy and incoherent. Chip took her to the emergency room and she was admitted to the hospital at 3am.

Various tests, CAT scans, MRI scans, spinal tap, EEG – all came back normal – yet, Lynda was continuing to have frequent episodes (about 10 minutes apart). As the neurologist observed Lynda during the EEG (which showed normal activity), she declared that Lynda was having a petit mal seizure and ordered steroids and anti-convulsive medication.

During the next few days, more tests were done and doctors scrambled to try and find what was causing the extreme, sudden downward spiral in Lynda's condition. Lynda had begun showing symptoms of aphasia (a language disorder caused by damage to the brain) – the inability to recall names and nouns -- almost immediately.

Chip stayed with her around the clock until she was transferred to the NICU on the evening of April 27. Before he left, he said, "I told her that I wasn't allowed to stay in the hospital with her, but I would be staying at Jenny's house just a few miles away. She seemed to understand what I told her and I finished by holding her face in my hands and saying 'baby, I don't know what is going to happen over the next few days or weeks, but I want you to know that no matter what happens, I love you more than anything else in the world, and I always will. Please remember that, OK?' She responded with her wonderful smile, a hug and a great kiss. We prayed together, she cautioned me to be careful, and kissed me good-bye. As I walked away and looked back at her, she was holding her hand in the "I love you" sign she was known for."

"As I left the hospital, I had no way of knowing that it would be a long, long time until I would see her that coherent again. I had no way of knowing that we were embarking on a journey that would change our lives forever."

The next morning when he returned at 8am, Chip found Lynda unresponsive. A CAT scan indicated her brain was swelling and new medication was begun.

Chip said, "When I went into the hospital chapel to pray, I questioned God, 'Why her?' A hospital chaplain asked me if her sin was any better or worse than anyone else's. I responded that sin was sin in the eyes of God. He then stated, 'Then, why *not* her?' He was right."

Over the next weeks, Lynda's condition worsened, not only with the life-threatening brain swelling, but also blood clots in both arms and a leg and a myriad of other serious issues.

After three weeks of testing, the doctors determined her condition was caused by herpes 1 simplex viral encephalitis. The determination was made by process of elimination since this diagnosis was not indicated by any of the tests.

Improvement was slow. She was sleeping a lot and not very alert, but she did seem to understand what they said to her. Chip said, "One evening I wrote the word 'Jesus' on a white board and asked her what it said. She fell asleep before answering, but the next morning she told me, 'the word was Jesus.'"

Nearly six weeks after being admitted into the NICU, Lynda was still physically unstable, but considered neurologically stable enough to be transferred to the general ICU. Chip said, "She could not articulate any real memory of me or our daughter, or our past, but she could understand simple conversation – and we were excited to see her show occasional glimpses of being the 'old Lynda.'"

Chip said, "After Lynda was transferred to a rehab unit, each Sunday afternoon, I put her in a wheelchair and took her to the hospital chapel. There I would read some scripture to her, pray with her and sing to her. Although my singing has never been good, she always enjoyed the one hymn I could sort of sing well, 'Amazing Grace.'"

On August 7, 2007, over three months after their saga started, Lynda was discharged and taken home. Their journey toward recovery, however, had only just begun.

After more than a year of occupational therapy, speech therapy and physical therapy, a broken arm from a fall, a hysterectomy, removal of gall bladder and treatment for ulcers, Lynda was finally able to regain enough independence to stay by herself during the day. In the spring of 2008, Chip took her for therapy at the InterAct Program for Communication in Halifax, Nova Scotia, where she made remarkable progress. She has returned there several more times.

As the year 2008 continued, Chip said, "During this time period we started to better develop our lives. We went back to many of the things we used to do together (dinner, shopping, visiting with our daughter. now our granddaughter as well, church functions, etc.). I started to go back into some of my hobbies (flight instructing, church board activities, school board activities, etc.). This made Lynda very happy as her main goal then and now remains to make sure we are as 'normal as possible' and that I can do the same type of things that I used to do. Lynda is very motivated by this desire, which is not unlike the way we were before her illness (each very motivated by making the other one happy).

By April 2013, six years after the event that changed their lives, Lynda was enjoying a large degree of independence, including driving along familiar streets. In spite of the limitations she still lived with, Lynda continued to live by her long time attitude, saying, "If you can't be thankful for what you have, at least be thankful for what you don't have."

They had survived a traumatic life-changing tragedy and come through it – not unscathed, but still kicking. Chip quotes words from the framed statement by Chuck Swindoll that he has hanging over his desk for many years, "'*Life is 10% what happens to you and 90% what you do with it.*' That 90% takes a strong faith in God and desire to make the very best out of the situation."

April 30, 2013, the unthinkable happened, and the ax fell for the second time. On that day, Chip did what Chip does: he stopped along the side of the highway to help a person in distress. He is the epitome of a Good Samaritan (he's been involved in helping people with Angel Flights for over 20 years). As he stood in the wide grassy median area with a distressed driver, an oncoming truck slid off the road and collided with both Chip and the driver. As the truck hit Chip, it ripped his right leg off just above the knee.

Chip said, "When I hit the ground and saw my leg lying 20 feet away, I knew in that moment that I was suddenly an amputee. The first thing I thought about was what the doctor told my father when his leg had been run over by a train when I was eleven years old and he nearly died. I felt God had prepared me for this accident. I remember the doctor telling my father he'd lived because he remained conscious. I knew I had to make it for Lynda, because she needed me. I didn't lose consciousness until they put me under at the hospital."

As it had been with Lynda's illness, so it was with Chip's tragedy – complications ensued. His heart had to be shocked twice to bring him back, he developed sepsis, and he had 30 surgical procedures within the first two months.

After Chip's recovery, he said, "Do I like it? No! But, my life is not over. I'm not a saint – I have moments and allow myself five minutes to feel sorry for myself." He laughs. "I actually time myself and then I say, I'm done. It is what it is. Things happen and you have to deal with them."

Throughout his recovery, Lynda was by his side – just as he'd been by her side years earlier. Roles were reversed, and for a while, Lynda became the caretaker. She still has difficulty with some words and could not think of the word "caretaker." Both she and Chip have a great sense of humor, so we all chuckled as she said, "Even though I can't say the word, I can do it."

Just a year after the loss of his leg, Chip was wearing a prosthesis, playing golf with his friends from church. He is thankful that, as a deacon in the church, he has been able to serve the Lord's Supper – first from his wheelchair, then with a cane, and now fully walking.

He says, "Every day is a gift from God. I really value life tremendously. All these things did was reinforce that. I tell people, every morning, I see the green side of the grass – not the brown side. I still have Lynda and I get to kiss her each night."

Because of what they have been through, both Lynda and Chip have been able to help others. Her doctor sees Lynda as "a poster child for aphasia recovery." Chip said, "Through her illness, we have come in contact with 60-70 couples with aphasia and we've been able to help them. Her recovery has offered motivation for others with aphasia."

Chip has done his part as well, helping encourage amputees and give them pointers on how to better manage their situation. "I would not have chosen these things to happen," said Chip, "but since they've occurred, we've had such blessings and been able to help people. I don't think God causes things to happen like this, but He uses them to His benefit. I don't want to let Him down."

When Chip speaks of Lynda, he calls her his hero. He says, "She is a loving, caring, dedicated wife, mother and grandmother, with a deep sense of God and obligation. Even when she was far from being well, one item of normalcy that never seemed to leave was her faith and love for God. Every night before we went to sleep, we held hands and prayed, much as we did before she got sick and while she was in the hospital. Each night she tried her part of the prayer. Much of her prayer was understandable even though the right words were not used. She consistently prayed for me, our daughter and granddaughter Gracie. I knew the words weren't quite right, but I also knew that God understood them all."

As far as the "new normal" in their lives – Chip says, "We have to compensate for our frailties. We all have them. My philosophy is – do what you can, not what you can't. Through it all, the important thing is the same thing it takes in marriage – full trust in each other and full faith in Christ."

Lynda adds, "You don't give up, you go forward – and remember, God is number one in all of this."

Lynda's life verse: *"Be still and know that I am God"* Psalm 46:10
Chip's life verse: *"And the peace of God, which surpasses all understanding, will guard your hearts and minds through Christ Jesus"* Philippians 4:7

-Photo: Courtesy photo of a portion of the Blanton Elementary fifth grade class.

FINDING STRENGTH IN GOD'S WORD

We've read the stories of these dear sisters, ordinary women like you and me. We've cried over their pain and loss, laughed at their humorous tidbits, rejoiced in their victories and, hopefully, whispered a prayer for those who are still going through the floodwaters.

While their words are meant to inspire and encourage us, it is God's Word that we can hold onto when all else fails us. Our extraordinary God's love for us is beyond our understanding, but so treasured in our heart of hearts. He alone can complete us and fulfill our deepest needs.

> *"My heart is overflowing with a good theme; I recite my composition concerning the King; my tongue is the pen of a ready writer"* Psalm 45:1

Let's view our extraordinary God as the Sovereign Creator that He is – the great Potter who offers us the all-surpassing treasure of His indwelling Spirit.

We'll pop in on Abraham and Isaac during the hardest moments of their lives and be reminded that God's viewpoint is the one that truly matters.

We're reminded that *fear* is one of Satan's favorite tools. We need to recognize his manipulations and call out to God for peace.

Tears are the language of the heart – whether in joy or sorrow.

Always, God promises that His Grace is Sufficient and that He gives strength in time of trouble.

Beauty from Ashes is one of the wonderful promises from our loving God and something to remember when we're going through the floodwaters.

So, let's plunge into the next section and discover some of the wonderful facets of our most extraordinary God and Father.

SOVEREIGN GOD

"For I am God, and there is no other;
I am God, and there is none like Me" Isaiah 46;9

How often in the midst of a problem do we say, "I don't understand!" There are so many things in this world that we don't understand, and "Why do bad things happen to good people?" is among the most frequently asked question of them all. We just don't understand how and why tragedy strikes as it does.

The thing is – we're not required to understand these things. In fact, not understanding is often part of the process of what we must go through. Hebrews 11:1 reminds us, *"Now faith is the substance of things hoped for, the evidence of things not seen."* Faith is trusting in something – or more specifically – in Someone whom we cannot see. If we understood everything that's happening, it would not leave room for Faith – and Faith in a sovereign, all-knowing, loving God is what it's all about.

Is Faith an easy road to follow? That would be a big NO – in all caps. Is it worth the effort? That would be an equally big YES – in all caps.

~Sovereign God

When God spoke to Isaiah in 55:9, He pointed out: *"For My thoughts are not your thoughts, nor are your ways My ways, says the Lord. For as the heavens are higher than the earth, so are My ways higher than your ways, and My thoughts than your thoughts."*

God offers the most startling contrast between Himself and man by way of how infinitely above us He is in every way. As we all know, the heavens are so vast that even planets are light years away from our earth - and, we've never even mapped the entire universe (and I don't believe we ever will!). That gives us a glimpse of the overwhelming truth of how much higher God's ways are than our ways. He is so much more than we can ever be that we cannot even comprehend the vast gulf between our ways and His ways.

And yet, we tend to feel the need to try and understand all He is doing in our lives – especially when something painful and incomprehensible is happening. We ask, "Why?" and search for answers to the reason behind it all. If we would take to heart that verse in Isaiah we would realize that we are not privy to God's reasons and we are not required to know the answers. We are, however, expected to trust in the One who is in control of it all and knows the end from the beginning – and everything in between. Trusting in what we cannot see or understand – that's the definition of Faith.

~Job's Questions

Job didn't understand why God allowed all the tragedy that crashed down on him that day so long ago. In the midst of his sorrows, his faith faltered. In chapters 27-31, Job speaks of all the ways he'd sought to live a righteous life and how he just didn't deserve all this horror surrounding him. He said, *"When I looked for good, evil came to me; and when I waited for light, then came darkness"* 30:26. He didn't understand why so many bad things were happening to him – a good man. As he poured out his heart to God, he said, *"Oh, that the Almighty would answer me..."* 31:35.

Well, the Lord did answer him. The Lord appeared in a whirlwind and set Job straight in chapters 38-41. I can almost hear the voice of God booming out as the wind swirled and Job was probably thinking he should have been more careful what he asked for. I can imagine him hiding his head in fear as God vividly recounted wonder after wonder that He had created, things like:

Have you entered the treasury of snow? By the breath of God ice is given, and the broad waters are frozen.

Where were you when I laid the foundations of the earth? Tell me, if you have understanding.
Can you bind the cluster of Pleiades...?
Can you pour out the bottles of heaven, when the dust hardens in clumps...? Where is the way to the dwelling of light?
God asked Job, "*Shall the one who contends with the Almighty correct Him?*" 40:1

    Ouch! I think that last question God asked might be one of our problems as well. When we question God and say, 'Oh, that's not fair, or I don't deserve that, or why me, God, and why this?' Are we, like Job, trying to correct the almighty, sovereign God, and tell Him that He should have done it differently?

    I confess, I'm guilty of trying to tell God what to do at times. I wince at writing those words, but it's the truth and we can't hide the truth from God. We all do it. We pray, asking God to do this and this and this, and we don't understand why He doesn't follow our game plan.

    Then, when things sometimes go from bad to worse, we really throw a hissy fit – 'Lord, have you forgotten that I'm your child? Why are you treating me like this? Why are you allowing this tragedy to descend upon me?'

    Well, don't beat yourself up if you've found yourself in that situation. As you can see, Job did the same thing and – even though God let him know in no uncertain terms that HE was God, not Job – even then, God was merciful to His son, forgave his effrontery, and ended up blessing Job abundantly.

    Don't forget, Job also humbly apologized to God. Then Job answered the Lord: "*I am unworthy – how can I reply to you? I put my hand over my mouth. I spoke once, but I have no answer – twice, but I will say no more.*"

    And then, after God has spoken to Job again, Job replies to the Lord: "*My ears had heard of You, but now my eyes have seen You...*" 42:5.

    Can you say with Job, "*My ears had heard of You, but now my eyes have seen You...*" OR must you say, "*My ears had heard of You, but I have not yet seen You...I do not know You.*"

    God's dearest desire is for you and I to know Him – to see Him for what He is – the sovereign God of the universe who is our gracious, amazing Father who as Jeremiah reminds us, *"loves us with an everlasting love."*

~Almighty & All-Powerful

While the sovereignty of God should be frightening and intimidating, it should also be comforting and thrilling. You say, how can it be both? Almighty God rightly deserves our complete awe and respect and worship and, yes, even fear in the right sense. But, He is also our loving, comforting Father and it is thrilling to watch Him work on the behalf of His beloved children (that would be you and me).

It is so exciting to see Him work. Remember, He made all of the worlds, He controls every atom and nanosecond, and He can change the laws of nature to suit His supernatural plans. Have you seen God's supernatural Hand at work? I have, and let me tell you, it is EXCITING – in all caps!

God's sovereignty is evident throughout scripture. His strength overcomes -- whether by many or a few. He delights in displaying His power by way of the few and the weak. He knows it brings delight, encouragement and hope to His children as well. Here are a few of God's wonderful promises from Psalms:

"A thousand may fall at your side, and ten thousand at your right hand; but it shall not come near you" 91:7.

"Some trust in chariots, and some in horses; but we will remember the name of the LORD our God" 20:7

"God is our refuge and strength, a very present help in trouble./ Therefore we will not fear, even though the earth be removed, and although the mountains be carried into the midst of the sea" 46:1-2.

"The nations raged, the kingdoms were moved; He uttered His voice, the earth melted" 46:6.

"In God I have put my trust; I will not be afraid. What can man do to me?" 56:11

I don't think God expects us to be the first in line to sign up for tragedy and devastation. I do believe that He wants us to *"Be still"* and know that He is God – and to trust Him with whatever He allows into our lives. Sarah Young wrote in *Jesus Calling*, "You will never be in control of your life circumstances, but you can relax and trust in My control."

~He is the Potter

We must never forget that God is the One who created you and me and, therefore, we are His to do with as He sees fit. I'm so thankful He loves us, so that we can trust what He does is for the best.

Since He is the Potter and we are the clay, it's His right to make one a simple bowl, another a cup or plate, while He might choose to make someone else into a fine vase or a lovely urn. We must be aware that He has complete control – whether we like it or not. What He wants from us is submission. He longs for His creation to acknowledge Him and bow to His sovereign will. When we do, He will bless us with such joy.

Paul writes to the Romans about this issue, "*But indeed, O man, who are you to reply against God? Will the thing formed say to Him who formed it, 'Why have you made me like this?' / Does not the potter have power over the clay, from the same lump to make one vessel for honor and another for dishonor?*" 9:20-21.

Isaiah also writes about God being the Potter: "*But now, O Lord, You are our Father; we are the clay, and You our Potter; and all we are the work of Your hand*" 64:8.

One of my favorite verses has to do with the fact that we are clay formed by the Potter and the beauty of being that "jar of clay" is that He has given us the amazing privilege of being His vessel and we carry within us the greatest treasure imaginable.

What is that treasure? It is the all-surpassing power of the Holy Spirit of God Himself. "*But we have this treasure in jars of clay to show that this all-surpassing power is from God and not from us*" 2 Corinthians 4:7. Let that sink in. As Christians, we have the Holy Spirit of God living within ourselves every minute of every day. And – that Holy Spirit has power that surpasses all other power.

That same all-powerful Spirit that lives within my heart and mind also lives within your heart and mind if you are saved. He also lives in the hearts and minds of all the millions of others of His children. Imagine it like an invisible cord between each of us, drawing us together -- revealing to someone you've never met that you are both one in the Spirit; impressing upon your heart to speak a word to a brother or sister that they need to hear. The Holy Spirit works in miraculous, mysterious and amazing ways within us. What a joy to be a vessel housing this all-surpassing power!

Would you want the job of running this entire world and every person living here? Me neither! I am so thankful that God is God and I am His beloved little jar of clay. Thank you, dear Lord!

"Blessed be the name of God forever and ever, for wisdom and might are His, and He changes the times and the seasons; He removes kings and raises up kings; He gives wisdom to the wise and knowledge to those who have understanding. / He reveals deep and secret things; He knows what is in the darkness, and light dwells with Him. I thank You and praise You, O God of my fathers….: Daniel 2:20-21.

-Photo: Like twigs dipped in crystal, these ice-encrusted branches displayed God's glory in Colonial Williamsburg, VA. SJB

TESTING—ONE, TWO, THREE

God said to Abraham: "Take now your son, your only son Isaac, whom you love, and go the land of Moriah, and offer him there as a burnt offering on one of the mountains of which I shall tell you" Genesis 22:2

Although our book is primarily about ordinary women, I want to include this story of an ordinary man who went through an extraordinary test that put a spotlight on our amazing, extraordinary God. We can learn much from this encounter that might help us understand a bit more about the inner workings of a test from God. If we can imagine what is going on behind the scenes in the invisible world, it might help bolster our faith and trust in our gracious unseen Father.

Most of us are familiar with the story of Abraham's obedience to God on the hilltop. We read the story and, as frightening as the thought of such a test is to us, we know the outcome and we're able to breathe a sigh of relief that a father did not have to kill his son. We see the test as a done-deal. We know those who were involved passed the test and were blessed as a result of their obedience. It might help us, however, to look deeper into the emotions and behind-the-scenes work that surrounded this intense episode in history.

Abraham, like his wife Sarai, was no super-Christian any more than you and I are. They were an ordinary man and woman whom our extraordinary God chose to use to reveal to us various facets of Himself and to further His kingdom on this earth. That's what He wants to do through you and I as well. Probably not on a world stage and to the extent He used Abraham and Sarai, but scope is not always what God is after in our individual lives. He seeks faithful servants in every corner of the world for both big and small jobs.

We're reminded by the very theme of this book that testing is one of the tools God uses to refine and teach His children. Observing the testing in another sister or brother's life can also be a learning tool for us. Let's see what we can learn from our brother Abraham's ultra-test.

From Heaven's view the world and all our experiences and testing looks very different than it does from our earthly viewpoint. Consider Abraham's dilemma on the hillside that day with his son Isaac. There was a lot going on in all the realms during that three-day period when the men were tramping along the trails seeking the spot God had chosen for the sacrifice. The outcome of that test on the hillside would be a pivotal moment in history. There are numerous viewpoints involved – let's look at five of those viewpoints.

~Our viewpoint: Let's consider our viewpoint as we search scripture and our imaginations, seeking understanding, purpose, meaning in this intense event that happened nearly 4,000 years ago. Our viewpoint is entirely different from the two men because we see the event as a whole and we know how the story ends. Not only that, but we've also seen God's hand at work throughout the intervening years of history, and we have an entire Bible that has revealed so much about God and His work to us since that time. We've seen the heart of God through His Son Jesus and His great sacrifice for which this test was an early picture, and we have the indwelling Holy Spirit as our permanent helper.

In spite of all this, I wonder how you or I would have responded to such a test?

~Abraham's viewpoint: Let's examine Abraham's viewpoint as he struggles with obedience in a situation that doesn't make sense to him. During that three-day trip, don't you think he must have asked himself a hundred times, "Did I really hear God right on this? Why? How?"

This was a man who'd left home and family to follow after God to a distant land – in obedience to God's Word. He'd been through a lot in his desire to please God, even waiting 100 years before God sent to him that promised son, Isaac. Always, he'd sought to be obedient to the God he loved and served, but this – this was just so hard.

I can't even imagine being able to walk up the hill on that third day with the knowledge of what lay ahead, let alone raise the knife above the face of my beloved child and be ready to plunge that sharp blade into his precious body. Everything within us rebels at such an act. We ask ourselves, is there any way I could have done that?

I've heard preachers say that Abraham probably believed that God would immediately raise Isaac back to life, or something like that. Perhaps that faith helped him forge ahead, go up that hill, lay out the wood, tie up his son and raise the knife upward. Perhaps. We don't know.

Remember, this was an ordinary man – who loved God and sought to obey him as best he could much like you and I do – yet, I believe, this is a test beyond what an ordinary man or woman would be able to pass in his or her own strength. I believe that our extraordinary God gave Abraham the strength and faith to follow through and do the thing. In those moments when Abe's strength may have waned, God gave him a dose of supernatural sufficiency that said, *"I can do all things through Christ* [or God], *who strengthens me"* Philippians 4:13.

I believe this was the victory for Abraham as it will be for you and I when we are in the midst of a hard test -- that God infuses us with his extraordinary power and works a miracle in the hearts of His ordinary children.

~Isaac's viewpoint: Isaac's viewpoint is rarely considered in this scenario. If he were here today, he'd probably feel like saying, "Hello! What about me? I was there too. I was the intended victim, for pity sake!" The only mention of Isaac's reaction to the events was when he questions his father about the missing sacrifice: *"Look, the fire and the wood, but where is the lamb for a burnt offering?"*

It's not surprising that Isaac easily accepts his father's explanation that *"God will provide for Himself the lamb for a burnt offering."* This young man had probably developed a faith of his own, taught by his Father, and learned through his own experiences with God in the desert.

What I find hard to fully imagine, however, is this teenage boy allowing his father to tie him up, place him on an uncomfortable wooden altar and raise a knife over his head without a peep. Isaac must have thought his father had gone mad by now, yet there is no indication of a struggle from him.

Here we have a young guy who is the beloved, honored son – the very heartbeat of his Mother and Father – and his Dad is about to kill him.

I'm at a loss to explain Isaac's docile behavior. Since scripture doesn't offer us any further information on the subject, all I can do is shrug my shoulders and know that God is in control of all things and He took care of the situation.

~Satan's viewpoint: What do you think that looked like? Satan is well-acquainted with God and His Holiness and His love and character. Don't forget, Satan does not know the future, nor is he all-powerful, all-knowing or all-present as God is. Satan's powers are limited, nonetheless, he is still very powerful and crafty. I believe there was an intense spiritual battle waging along that path and up on the hillside during that test period.

Satan can only be in one place at a time and although he is not mentioned in this test, you can count on him being there. I believe this test was so important to God's enemy that he was probably on that path with Abraham for three solid days, and then on the hilltop, invisibly yelling into the soul of God's servant not to trust in a God who would require his own son as a sacrifice.

Satan is usually eager for blood, but in this case, I don't think he wanted blood to flow. If Abraham had plunged that knife into his son's chest, I think perhaps it might have been a victory for Satan on some level, but if Abraham had stopped at some point and said, "I just can't do it, God. I'm not gonna trust you on this one" – that would have been the greater victory for Satan. He may have seen that moment on the hilltop as a win-win for the dark side.

I love the way God always foils Satan's plans. No matter how dark the hour, God always shines His light on the issue and brings good out of evil. He never fails and Satan never gets the best of Him. God's timing is not always our time, but it always turns out to be the right time.

In the case of Abraham's test, timing was crucial and as always, God was right on time. Can you imagine the surprise on Satan's face when the event played out as it did and a ram showed up at just the right moment?

Foiled again!

~Then, there was God. There is always God and it's His viewpoint that rules the world. That's why if we can get a glimpse of life from His exalted view, it will be easier for us to survive what Pastor Frye calls, "the hard vicissitudes of life."

God had His almighty hand on Abraham's pulse every step of the way along that path and up the hill. God knew every emotion, question and doubt. I believe He watched as His beloved son struggled intensely with these emotions and questions. From our viewpoint thousands of years later, we can see that God had a plan all along. He knew Abraham would obey Him; He knew Isaac was safe; He led the ram into the thicket at just the right time. God could calmly and lovingly watch the scene unfold because He knew the outcome and He had a purpose for everything that happened.

Now, let's try to see this scene from God's view and imagine one of the purposes for all of it. Was the purpose of the test to see if Abraham would obey God?

No, at least not from God's viewpoint. God knew that Abraham would obey Him before the test was even begun. Remember, God knows the future just as well as He knows the past and everything in between.

So – who needed to know that Abraham would obey God in the most difficult test of his life? Abraham needed to know. Knowing he passed the hardest test he would probably ever face gave him a strength and knowledge in his faith in God – and in God's love and mercy -- that can only come through such testing.

Testing is not to show God what we'll do, but to show us how we will respond. Will we respond with obedience and praise, or will we fail to trust and choose our own way for the outcome?

No one ever said testing was easy, but the eternal reward for passing beats an "A" on earth by light years.

Here's a glimpse of Abraham's reward for passing the test: *"By Myself I have sworn, says the Lord, because you have done this thing, and have not withheld your son, your only son – blessing I will bless you, and multiplying I will multiply your descendants as the stars of the heaven and as the sand which is on the seashore; and your descendants shall possess the gate of their enemies. In yours all the nations of the earth shall be blessed, because you have obeyed My voice"* Genesis 22:16-18.

-Photo: Two little lambs were enjoying the rich green grass in a field we stopped by in Scotland. They're so adorable! SJB

FEARS

"God has not given us the spirit of fear, but of power and of love and of a sound mind" 2 Timothy 2:7

Fear is one of Satan's favorite tools. He and his followers use it without mercy every single day of every single year. We know there have to be valleys and dark times in our lives, but we don't know when or how bad they will be – and we don't know who it might affect. Will it be one of my children or grandchildren? My spouse or dear one? My parents? My sister or brother or best friend? Or, will it be me?

When do we fear? We fear when things are going good – we wonder -- when will the ax fall? And -- we fear when things are going bad and wonder how much worse they might get. Huh! Guess that means we are candidates for a hearty dose of fear anytime and anyplace and at regular intervals.

There is also that subtle fear that creeps in at random times and lodges at the edge of our minds and hearts – just a little thing, like a speck of sand in your shoe that rolls around under your foot.

Satan and his demons are equipped with a quiver full of hateful sins that they shoot at us like deadly arrows on a daily basis. They lodge in our hearts and minds causing pain along with fear, guilt, jealousy, pride, lust, greed – the list is long and their quivers are overflowing.

In this chapter, we're keying in on the arrow of fear. I'm sick of fear having so much sway in my life and I'm sure you feel the same way. Like Jennifer Rothchild wrote in one of her Bible studies, "Girl, the battle is always spiritual."

~A Spiritual Battleground

When it comes to fear, no matter the direction it's coming from, it usually boils down to a spiritual battle. The verse in Timothy makes it plain that fear does not originate with God, therefore, it must originate with Satan which means a battleground is somewhere in the picture.

We fear so many things – we fear the possibility of sickness, we fear the possibility of death, we fear the possibility of losing the person we love most in some way, we fear the possibility of failure, pain – you name it, we fear it. The strange thing is that most of the things we fear never come to pass. We live in a state of fear on such a regular basis that we often don't even realize that it's there coloring every thought and every move.

I want to share an attack of fear that came upon me one afternoon – out of the blue and for no good reason. I call it an "attack of fear" because it all had to do with manipulation of my imagination. It had nothing to do with a real event. Although it happened twenty years ago, the intensity of the incident was so strong that it stands out in my memory as if it happened yesterday. See if this strikes a chord in your own memory vault of fear.

~Attacked by Fear

It was Wednesday evening and I was getting into the car to drive to Prayer Meeting at church when the attack began. My sixteen-year old daughter Holly had left earlier to drive 20 miles through rush hour interstate traffic to an acting class she was taking.

As I pulled from my driveway, I suddenly saw a picture in my mind of my beautiful, beloved daughter lying on the side of the road after a terrible car accident. The more I "looked" at this scene, the more details of her horrible condition were shown to me. I won't go into what I "saw," but seeing my precious little girl in that condition truly broke my heart.

In a matter of seconds, fear shot through me like a raging inferno. My heart was pounding and I started weeping uncontrollably.

As I write this, tears stream down my face just remembering the fearful images I "saw" and the heartbreak I went through during that ten minute drive to church. The evil ones who put these visions into my mind raked me over the coals with such intensity I've never forgotten a minute of that imagined tragedy.

When I arrived at church, I dried my eyes and slipped into a back pew. With my heart still pounding with fear, in that moment, it immediately dawned upon me that I was under demonic attack. I felt shock at the realization. I had been so caught up in fear I'd failed to see it for what it was – satanic manipulation of a child of the King. In that split second, I rebuked the dark forces in the name of Jesus and prayed for Jesus to protect Holly and to take away my fear. The swiftness of the Lord's answer to my prayer was so instantaneous, I still marvel at it.

Jesus immediately took away my fear, stilled my racing heart and gave me peace about Holly's safety. Right then and there in the space of a heartbeat my fear was gone and the demons were banished. It was a beautiful moment!

~Important Truths

In that brief incident (no more than ten minutes long), I experienced an intense demonic attack that was revealed to me by the Lord Himself. I discovered several vastly important truths – one truth being that demonic attacks of fear are real and powerful, but praise God, *"Greater is He that is within me than He that is in the world"* 1 John 4:4.

A second important truth is that it is not God that gives us that spirit of fear, because He has said we are not to fear. Over and over in scripture God tells us to "Fear not." Instead, we are to trust God. When we trust God, we are not overcome by fear. Trusting God and fearing not go together; it is Satan who is big on spreading fear. One of his biggest goals is to damage or better yet, destroy, a Christian's trust in God's promised watch-care over us.

As I mentioned before, fear is one of Satan's favorite tools and since God does not give us that spirit of fear, it always comes from the demon side of the realm. So, to say the battle is nearly always spiritual is absolutely true when fear is the culprit.

I'm not saying that every bout of fear is a demonic attack. I believe there are times when a fearful thought pops into our minds that it is our own flawed human nature that prompted the thought, but I do believe that most of our bouts of fear, especially those featuring vivid pictures of horrific events playing out in your mind in living color, are sent by demons. It makes me angry to think these vile creatures can get away with such manipulation.

We don't have to let them have this much control of our lives. If you daily ask the Holy Spirit to guide and guard your thoughts, you'll be surprised how much it helps. Then, times when those wily minions still manage to get through, we need to be aware of what they're doing and quickly call on Jesus to subdue them and fill us with peace to replace fear.

Another very important truth is that the vast majority of our fears never come to pass. Fear is a combination of chemical reactions and imagination (fueled by you know who) that has little to do with reality. Certainly, the reality we see in circumstances and news reports around us cloud our vision and color our thoughts. This is where imagination can take wing and paint fearful scenarios into our minds. These scenarios are not reality. Repeat along with me – "the vast majority of our fears never come to pass."

~Peace and Victory
The last part of that verse in 2 Timothy tells us what God lovingly offers us in the place of fear and what God graciously and immediately provided for me when I called upon His name. By His love, He gave me the power to stop a demonic attack in its tracks and as a result, He gave me a sound mind that was no longer traumatized by an imagined, fake tragedy.

I'm thankful God allowed me to go through that event. I can just imagine the demons getting permission to attack me and bringing me to the point of being a quivering mass of tears and terror. They were probably laughing and feeling all victorious. Then, the Holy Spirit lets me know what's happening and empowers me to toss those evil entities out the window. The peace and victory – and new knowledge that resulted from that attack was, I believe, the reason God allowed it in the first place.

Ah, the beauty of it -- God had a purpose and a good ending in mind all along.

Don't let the demon "What if…" worm his way into your day and rob you of peace.

~God in Control
We don't always get to see a beginning and end to a learning event from God in such a short period of time, but if you keep your spiritual eyes and ears open, such learning events probably happen a lot more frequently than you realize. He is in control of every atom and nanosecond and every shred of everything there ever was and ever will be – and He is busy weaving meaning and purpose into all of it.

> *"For I know the plans I have for you"* declares the Lord,
> *"plans to prosper you and not to harm you,*
> *plans to give you hope and a future"* Jeremiah 29:11

TEARS

"You number my wanderings; put my tears into Your bottle; are they not in Your book?"
Psalm 56:8

It was the custom in ancient times for people to actually save their tears in bottles. When we were in Rhodes, Greece, I saw a collection of these ancient alabaster tear bottles (pictured below) and imagined women holding the smooth opening up to their eyes as they cried. The tears would, of course, evaporate over time and probably leave a salty residue, even so, they seemed to treat their tears as tiny treasures to hold onto.

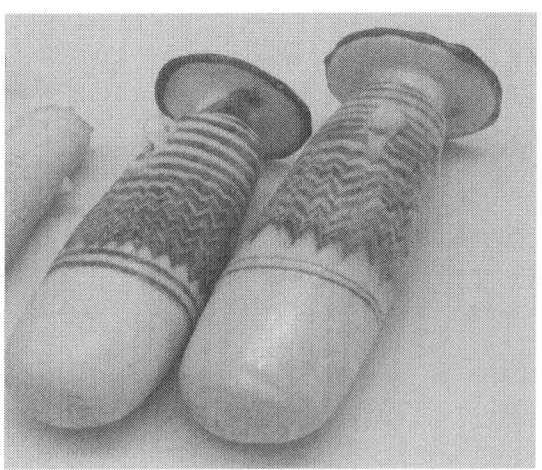

Ancient tear bottles

~Boo-hoo

For years, it bothered me that I cry so easily. When my heart is touched (and my heart is easily touched), I usually tear up and often outright weep. It can be embarrassing when I'm trying to tell a story or give a prayer request. There are many reasons for a woman's tears – both negative and positive. There are tears of sorrow, anger, fear, pain, and even the straw-that-broke-the-camels-back kind of tears that happen when you've reached the end of your rope. Sometimes when we're stressed out, a good cry is almost like a reset button for our hearts and minds. It's a cathartic exercise that can do a world of good. On occasion, I've found relief in such tears.

~Language of the Heart
The tears that I have come to embrace are tears that flow when I'm lost in praise to almighty God. I frequently cry during my times alone with God because I am so deeply moved by my encounters with Him. After pondering my propensity for weeping, I realized that my tears are a form of praise to God and I believe He is pleased by them. They are a language of the heart that cannot be put into words. Indeed, I believe He puts them into His spiritual tear bottle and counts them as precious in His sight. So, go ahead and let those tears flow, girls.

~Tears of Joy
It seems strange, but sometimes tears flow from joy and relief. I want to share an answer to prayer I had recently. I'd been searching for my bi-focal glasses for a couple days with no success. I'd only had them for a month or so and they were expensive - as all prescription glasses are - so I really needed to find them.

I decided to search the car for the fourth time. As I opened the car door, I prayed, "Please, Lord, help me find the glasses." Immediately, I reached under the seat and felt the glasses on the floor. My response to God's goodness was to burst into tears. Sounds strange, I know, but these were tears of praise at the wonder of God. I cried out, "Thank you, Father!"

I felt truly humbled by His grace and thankful for His kindness to me. I had a little praise party right there on the driveway -- complete with waterworks!

~Tears of Sorrow
The tears that are hardest to endure are surely tears of intense sorrow and loss. At such times, you may feel you could almost drown in your tears, there is such a flood. There is a song by Laura Story, "Blessings," that speaks of that hard to understand way that God sometimes works – through hard, painful times. The song reminds us that God works in mysterious ways in our lives and sometimes He sends blessings through raindrops.

According to medical science, emotional tears are actually helpful for our body, because harmful chemicals are released in the tears. The chemical involvement in crying is complex and is proven to relieve stress and help heal the body.

An interesting statistics shows that on average, women cry 47 times a year and men cry 7 times a year.

It's surprising, but sometimes when I have tears in my eyes, my vision is actually clearer. I look outside and see distant objects perfectly clear when normally I need eyeglasses to see that well. I think that physical anomaly offers a deeper spiritual meaning. There are many times that God provides us with clearer vision of an event or circumstance when we have tears in our eyes. Tears and the softening of the heart they represent allows God to speak to us in ways we might otherwise miss. Whether they are tears of sadness or gladness, thank God for the tears -- for they are precious in His sight.

The reasons for tears range from sorrow and devastating loss all the way to joy and wonder, with lots of gradient reasons in between the two extremes. Regardless of the reason, tears are a product of the earth and when we as God's children are removed from this earth and ready to settle into our perfectly beautiful eternal life, He has promised to do something for us that is infinitely tender. It kind of reminds me of what our Moms and Dads did for us when we were little and we got hurt or felt sad and cried.

God has promised to do that for us. Just like a loving parent, scripture tells us that our Holy Father "...*will wipe away every tear*" Revelation 21:4.

-Photo: The two ancient tear bottles are on display in a museum in Rhodes, Italy. SJB

HIS GRACE IS SUFFICIENT

"My grace is sufficient for you, for My strength is made perfect in weakness" 2 Corinthians 12:9

Haven't we all seen people in tragic or even trying circumstances and we ask, "How does she manage to get through this thing with such grace? How can she stay strong and keep from losing it in the midst of all the pain and sorrow?"

~Grace When Needed

I've noticed that God gives His children the grace and strength to bear a sorrow at the time the sorrow comes upon them – not before. Oh, He may prepare us for the upcoming sorrowful event with perhaps a pertinent sermon or Bible study session or visit from a friend – something that feeds our souls and strengthens our spirits, but the necessary portion of grace and strength only come when the tragedy hits.

I've often heard people say that we aren't given "dying grace" until we're ready to die. I've humorously responded, "Well, that's a relief. I guess it's not my time to die, because I'm not feeling that grace yet."

God's word is replete with promises that He will be there when we need Him. As children of God, we know that He is with us always, but in times of distress, it's as if He gives us a double-portion of His Spirit. The apostle Paul encourages us, saying, *"Let us therefore come boldly to the throne of grace, that we may obtain mercy and find grace to help in time of need"* Hebrews 4:16.

~Power of Grace

Paul well knows the power of grace. The words in the verse at the top of the page were spoken to Paul by the Lord Himself after Paul pleaded with God to relieve him of the *"thorn in the flesh"* that had been plaguing him. Here is the full story in just four verses:

"And lest I should be exalted above measure by the abundance of the revelations, a thorn in the flesh was given to me, a messenger of Satan to buffet me, lest I be exalted above measure. Concerning this thing I pleaded with the Lord three times that it might depart from me. And He said to me, 'My grace is sufficient for you, for My strength is made perfect in weakness.' Therefore most gladly I will rather boast in my infirmities, that the power of Christ may rest upon me. Therefore I take pleasure in infirmities, in reproaches, in needs, in persecutions, in distresses, for Christ's sake. For when I am weak, then I am strong" 2 Corinthians 12:7-10

I think you would agree with me that most of us do not "take pleasure in infirmities...." It's not in our human DNA to actually enjoy pain and suffering (at least, not in sane humans). So, how can a very sane apostle Paul make such a statement?

I'm certainly not an authority on this subject, but it appears to me that since Paul was in the midst of this physical infirmity and to some degree of suffering, God gave him a sufficient portion of grace and a dose of supernatural strength that allowed him to live with the thing. And not just "live with it," but to feel the presence and power of God so infusing him that he was able to rejoice in the trade. He was basically trading health and freedom from pain for the amazing presence and awesome power of the Spirit of almighty God resting upon and within him.

Paul saw the trade being in his favor and he lets us know that he took pleasure in it. This is a two thousand year old testimony that is sent to encourage our hearts when we find ourselves in tragic or even just trying circumstances.

~Strength for the Weary

Long before Paul arrived on the scene, a prophet named Isaiah testified of God's ability to work through that which is weak with His supernatural power. *"He gives strength to the weary and increases the power of the weak. Even youths grow tired and weary, and young men stumble and fall; but those who hope in the LORD will renew their strength. They will soar on wings like eagles; they will run and not grow weary, they will walk and not be faint"* Isaiah 40:29-31.

It would be delightful to *soar on wings like an eagle*. What a liberating and beautiful feeling that would be. But, if I don't have the ability to actually fly, it would be nice to at least be able to run fast and far and not grow weary as I run. There are times though when even walking seems like an impossible feat. Sometimes it becomes a struggle just to put one foot in front of the other. At such times, it would be a relief just to be able to *walk and not be faint* – to get by from one moment to the next without melting to the floor because you have come to the end of yourself.

However, it is often when we come to the end of ourselves that God picks us up and helps us to walk – and when even walking becomes too difficult, He's promised to pick us up and carry us – "*As an eagle stirs up its nest, hovers over its young, spreading out its wings, taking them up, carrying them on its wings*" Deuteronomy 32:11.

And so – even though we can barely walk, He picks us up and carries us on His wings as an eagle, thereby causing us to *soar on wings like an eagle*. What a beautiful picture! I don't know about you, but that picture brings tears to my eyes. Our God is so tender and loves us so much! He's not allowing these difficulties to come into our lives to break us, but rather to build us – and to draw us ever closer to His dear self.

I believe this is one of the pictures Paul may have seen as he clung to the Lord in his infirmity. Paul was in total agreement with the Psalmist when he said, "*The LORD is my strength and my shield; my heart trusts in Him, and I am helped. My heart leaps for joy and I will give thanks to Him in song. The LORD is the strength of His people, a fortress of salvation for His anointed one*" Psalm 28:7-8.

Oh, to be able to say both with Paul and the Psalmist, "...*my heart trusts in Him*..." And isn't that the key to it all – to trust the heart of our loving, generous, gracious heavenly Father who knows what is best for us through every smile and teardrop.

> *"And of His fullness we have all received, and grace for grace"* John 1:16

-Photo: The eagle picture is a bit blurry, because it was way high in the sky flying above the port of Ketchikan, Alaska as we stood on the deck of the ship getting ready to pull away from the dock. SJB

BEAUTY FOR ASHES

"...to give them beauty for ashes..." Isaiah 61:3

This is a powerful passage of scripture that God inspired Isaiah to write, it is rather lengthy, but well worth our time to read. May God speak to you through His Word.

> *"'The Spirit of the Sovereign Lord is on me, because the Lord has anointed me to preach good tidings to the poor.*
> *He has sent me to heal the brokenhearted, to proclaim liberty to the captives and the opening of the prison to those who are bound; to proclaim the acceptable year of the Lord, and the day of vengeance of our God; to comfort all who mourn, to console those who mourn in Zion – to give them beauty for ashes, the oil of joy for mourning, the garment of praise for the spirit of heaviness.*
> *That they may be called trees of righteousness, the planting of the Lord, that He may be glorified.' And they shall rebuild the old ruins, they shall raise up the former desolations and they shall repair the ruined cities, the desolations of many generations."*
> Isaiah 61:1-4 NKJ

There is a depth of sorrow and pathos in these verses that could break your heart, yet right alongside that pain, we see the healing hand of God lifting, planting, liberating. I weep for the pain and suffering these people went through – for their heaviness and the feeling that their whole lives had turned to ash, but trading that pain and the dry ashes for comfort and the rich oil of God's joy is surely worth it all.

> *"All who see them will acknowledge that they are a people the Lord has blessed"* 61:9 NIV

Throughout much of the Old Testament and even into the New Testament, reference to ashes is usually in a negative context. It offers an external sign of repentance – as in sackcloth and ashes, or of grief – often intense when ashes are thrown over the head and body. There is also reference to ashes as signifying that which is worthless – as in the things of the world that will be burned and turn to ash.

The Bible presents at least three separate pictures of ashes. At first glance, I saw the verses above as describing the second picture of ashes – that involving grief. Certainly, that is fully seen, but I think it goes deeper and can be seen to describe all three references to ashes before turning around and lifting the sufferers from their ashes to places of healing and victory.

~Ashes of Grief

I'm pulling this particular picture of ashes from the three listed above because I think it is something we need to be allowed to do without feeling guilty. When tragedy, sorrow, or loss come into your life, it's natural and even healthy (to a certain extent) to let yourself go through a period of grieving. It helps to fully express your sorrow and cry out to God, then to begin working through the issues, and eventually letting God heal your heart and bring that promised *"peace that passes understanding."*

You can't reach your destination of well-being by trying to take a detour around your grief. When one from ancient times experienced a loss, she tore her clothes, sprinkled ashes on her head and wailed out her grief – usually for days. While I don't recommend tearing your clothes – and where would we even find any ashes – the wailing part is something we sisters can usually do. In fact, it's a medical fact that crying actually removes harmful chemicals that build up in our bodies during times of emotional stress. Even Jesus wept from sorrow.

So, yes, let the tears flow and don't apologize. While the length of time for tears depends on the depth of your sorrow, there does come a time when tears need to be dried so that healing can begin. The Psalmist had much to say about crying and in chapter 30, he writes: *"O Lord my God, I cried out to You and you healed me….Weeping may endure for a night, but joy comes in the morning…You have turned for me my mourning into dancing…O Lord my God, I will give thanks to You forever."*

~Beauty for Ashes

After all the past suffering that's pictured in the verses, we have that beautiful phrase in the midst of the scripture passage, *"to give them beauty for ashes."*

I've heard it said that when a person's house burns down, it's one of the most desolate feelings you can experience when it comes to losing a possession. What happens when everything you worked for and cherished – everything inside your home and the very walls and roof that kept you warm and dry and safe – when it's all dry, smoldering ashes under your feet? What then?

That's the picture this verse represents. When we're surrounded by the ashes of heartbreak and sorrow, even death -- He has promised to replace it all with Beauty. And what is more beautiful than the Holy Spirit of God fulfilling your deepest need, wrapping you around with His comfort, and whispering His love into your heart. Now, that is a beautiful picture.

~~Overshadowing Beauty

Here's another beautiful picture: we were out west driving slowly along the back roads of one of the small towns in Montana. In the yard of a very modest little home sat the remains of an SUV. The back of the vehicle sat on cinder blocks and it was missing doors and fenders and – it basically looked stripped of everything that would have made it a functional vehicle. In spite of being an inanimate object, it looked sad.

Soaring above this pitiful shell was a beautiful tree with shining yellow leaves glowing in the sunlight. The contrast between the glorious tree and the sad car actually created a pleasing picture. The way the vibrant beauty of the tree overshadowed the ugliness of the poor vehicle reminds me of how God is able to make something beautiful out of even the most ugly. I love the verses in Isaiah 61 where He promises "*To give them beauty for ashes,*" and further also "*the garment of praise.*" And going along with our beautiful tree theme, He says, "*That they may be called trees of righteousness, the planting of the Lord, that He may be glorified.*"

That's what our Extraordinary God does for us, dear sister. He promises to give us beauty for ashes and the garment of praise. He has also promised that when He lifts us out of a horrible pit and out of miry clay, that He will set our feet upon a rock, establish our steps and put a new song in our hearts. Ah, now, that is a beautiful picture!

> "*He has put a new song in my mouth – praise to Our God; many will see it and fear, and will Trust In the Lord*" Psalm 40:3

The greatest aspect of the beauty of a new song, just like the beauty brought from ashes, is the fact that our Almighty, Loving Father of Grace reaches down into the hearts of we who are ordinary people – and He works a mighty work that only He could do – a work so mighty that those who see it in our lives will be amazed. As the Psalmist said, they will fear and they cannot help but believe in such a God as He.

It reminds me of a verse in Habakkuk 1:5. I'm taking it out of context, but I believe it might be applied here as well when God says, "*Be utterly astounded! For I will work a work in your days which you would not believe, though it were told you.*" I believe when God shows forth His extraordinary power and love and healing through the lives of His children – as He has in the lives of the women whose stories we've read in this book – that He works a work that is astounding. We cannot help but smile and even shake our heads in wonder at what our awesome God has accomplished – and continues to accomplish every day.

In every aspect, the many ups and downs in life that we experience are meant to produce glory to God -- and that is indeed our greatest and chief purpose. Praise God from whom all blessings flow!

> *"...And you shall be called the Repairer of the Breach, the Restorer of Streets to Dwell In"* Isaiah 58:12

Photo: The gorgeous yellow tree overshadowing the SUV shell was taken in a small town in Montana that we briefly passed through. SJB

THE LORD BLESS YOU AND KEEP YOU

*"The Lord bless you and keep you; the Lord make His face
To shine upon you, and be gracious to you; The Lord lift up His
Countenance upon you, and give you peace"*
Numbers 6:25-26

These words from Numbers were a blessing God laid upon the Children of Israel through the priests during the wilderness journey of His chosen people. He instructed Moses to tell the priests to offer this blessing *"So they shall put My name on the children of Israel, and I will bless them."*

Thousands of years later, Paul offered a similar benediction to the Christians at Corinth and it echoes that ancient blessing God gave to His children: *"Finally brethren, farewell. Become complete. Be of good comfort, be of one mind, live in peace; and the God of love and peace will be with you...The grace of the Lord Jesus Christ, and the love of God, and the communion of the Holy Spirit be with you all. Amen"* 2 Corinthians 13:11-14.

Maybe I'm getting too technical with the semantics and my own limited translations of scripture, but it appears to me that the early blessing was primarily laid upon the nation of Israel as a whole – that they would be "His people, called by His name." While the second blessing made after the death and resurrection of our Savior gives each of us as Christians the fullness of the Godhead as our source of blessing – a more personal indwelling that includes the communion of the Holy Spirit.

How blessed we are to be on this side of the cross of Christ, to be saved by grace and to have the most intimate of all relationships with the Almighty Himself – an indwelling of His very Spirit. When Paul writes, *"Be complete,"* He is reminding the Christians at Corinth and all of us who have ever named the name of Christ as Savior that He and He alone completes us. No person who walks upon this earth is capable of filling that role but God. There is such freedom and peace in that amazing knowledge.

And so, as a child of God, you and I can claim both blessings. With peace in our hearts and joy shining from our faces, we can lift up our eyes unto the hills and drink in the wonderful, supernatural blessings that God offers to us in both Numbers and Corinthians.

And so, I say to you, my sister, *"The Lord bless you and keep you. The Lord make His face to shine upon you and be gracious to you. The Lord lift up His countenance upon you -- and give you His wonderful peace that passes all understanding, in Christ Jesus...and the communion of the Holy Spirit be with you all."*

-Photo: The dove is part of a stained glass window depicting the day of Pentecost and represents the Holy Spirit coming upon the disciples with tongues of fire. The window is in the Seville Cathedral in Spain. SJB

SALVATION'S STORY

*"By grace are you saved through faith, and that not
of yourselves, it is the gift of God, not of works
lest anyone should boast"* Ephesians 2:8-9

I cannot write a book such as this without including the most important message of all – the Story God most wants us to hear – the gospel of Christ Jesus. Nothing in this world is as crucial to each and every person as accepting the gift of salvation offered to us by our Creator God.

In case you're not sure what that gift is or how to obtain it, here's the answer directly from His Word:

~Realize you are in need of salvation and cannot save yourself
--*"For all have sinned and fall short of the glory of God"* Romans 3:23.
--*"As it is written: There is no one righteous, not even one"* Romans 2:10.
--*"For the wages of sin is death, but the gift of God is eternal life in Christ Jesus our Lord"* Romans 6:23.
--*"Jesus said to him, 'I am the way, the truth, and the life. No one comes to the Father except through Me"* John 14:6.

~God Loves You and Christ Died for You
--*"For God so loved the world that he gave His one and only Son, that whoever believes in Him shall not perish but have eternal life"* John 3:16.

--*"But God demonstrated His own love for us in this; while we were still sinners, Christ died for us"* Romans 5:8.

~Good Works or Being Good Will not Save
--*"For it is by grace you have been saved, through faith – and this not from yourselves, it is the gift of God, not by works, so that no one can boast"* Ephesians 2:8-9.
--*"He saved us, not because of righteous things we had done, but because of His mercy. He saved us through the washing of rebirth and renewal by the Holy Spirit"* Titus 3:5.

~Salvation is a Gift We All Need
--*"Yet to all who received Him, to those who believed in His name, He gave the right to become children of God"* John 1:12.
--*"Jesus answered and said to him, 'Most assuredly, I say to you, unless one is born again, he cannot see the kingdom of God"* John 3:3.

~We Become New Creations When We are Born Again
--*"If you confess with your mouth, Jesus is Lord, and believe in your heart that God raised Him from the dead, you will be saved. For it is with your heart that you believe and are justified, and it is with your mouth that you confess and are saved"* Romans 10:9-10.
--*"Therefore, if anyone is in Christ, he is a new creation; the old has gone, the new has come!"* 2 Corinthians 5:17.

If you have never done so, I urge you with all my heart to accept this wonderful, free gift of salvation offered by a loving Father. I promise you that you will never regret making that choice – and that is a platinum-plated guarantee!

Photo: The realistic-looking statue of Jesus hanging on the cross can be found in Innsbruck, Austria, in a unique church called the Hofkirche. SJB

AUTHOR'S END NOTE

God has taught me that everything happens for a purpose. God allows, even orchestrates, difficult, heartbreaking, painful, tragic circumstances at certain times in our lives – because He loves us. We often don't realize it at the time, but the melody of our life is richer for the mournful bass notes used to accompany lighter tones of the treble cleft. The symphony of our lives is written by God -- not by ourselves. He is the Master writer and conductor. His is the genius behind the scenes. He alone knows the end from the beginning – and we must never forget that God Is Love. The view from Heaven is far different than the view from our earthly vision.

I hope this journey we've taken with ordinary women, just like ourselves, has given us a greater appreciation of not only what sisters throughout the ages have gone through, but even more so, for the extraordinary God that we are privileged to call Savior and Lord and Father. I pray God will bless your journey with Him – and if I don't have an opportunity to meet you here on earth, I look forward to meeting each of you in Heaven someday!

> *"Let the words of my mouth and the meditation of*
> *my heart be acceptable in Your sight, O Lord,*
> *my strength and my Redeemer"* Psalm 19:14

"Therefore we also, since we are surrounded by so great a cloud of witnesses, let us lay aside every weight, and the sin which so easily ensnares us, and let us run with endurance the race that is set before us, looking unto Jesus, the author and finisher of our faith..." Hebrews 12:1-2.

Your Sister in Christ, Sandra

Help from God's Extraordinary Word

Most of us take our Holy Bible for granted. We probably received a New Testament as a little child and we've owned one or more Bibles ever since. How many Bibles do you have in your home?

Throughout the ages of ancient times, God chose righteous men who were willing to be used by Him and He breathed His words into their minds and hearts. These men wrote what God impressed upon them as if He was dictating His message to them – Word for Word.

This book of scripture we hold in our hands is the very Word of the Almighty Creator of all – and He wants to speak to you and me through those pages. Let the wonder of it impress you anew with the unspeakable blessing of such a tremendous gift.

Here are some of His Words that He sent to encourage our hearts:

~Psalms Encouragement
The Psalms are full of wonderful encouragement – here are a few:

"Some trust in chariots, and some in horses; but we will remember the name of the Lord our God" 20:7.

"Hope in God; for I shall yet praise Him the help of my countenance and my God" Psalm 42:11.

"God is our refuge and strength, a very present help in trouble. Therefore we will not fear, even though the earth be removed, and though the mountains be carried into the midst of the sea; though its waters roar and be troubled, though the mountains shake with its swelling...God is in the midst of her, she shall not be moved" Psalm 46.

"He who dwells in the secret place of the Most High shall abide under the shadow of the Almighty. I will say to the Lord, 'He is my refuge and my fortress; My God, in Him I will trust.' He shall cover you with His feathers and under His wings you shall take refuge" Psalm 91.

"Bless the Lord, O my soul; and all that is within me, bless His holy name! Bless the Lord, O my soul, and forget not all His benefits..." 103:1-2.

"As a father pities his children, so the Lord pities those who fear Him. For He knows our frame; He remembers that we are dust" 103:13-14.

"He maketh the barren woman to keep house, and to be a joyful mother of children. Praise ye the Lord" 113:9 KJV.

"This is the day the Lord has made; we will rejoice and be glad in it" 118:24.

~Old Testament Promises are Ageless

"If my people who are called by My name will humble themselves, and pray and seek My face, and turn from their wicked ways, then I will hear from heaven, and will forgive their sin and heal their land" 2 Chronicles 7:14.

"...Lord, it is nothing for You to help, whether with many or with those who have no power, help us, O Lord our God, for we rest on You, and in Your name..." 2 Chronicles 14:11.

"Heal me, O Lord, and I shall be healed; save me, and I shall be saved, for You are my praise" Jeremiah 17:14.

"And you will seek Me and find Me, when you search for Me with all your heart. I will be found by you, says the Lord" Jeremiah 29:13-14.

"Call unto me and I will show you great and mighty things which you know not" Jeremiah 33:3.

"For I know the plans that I have for you, says the Lord, plans of peace and not of evil, to give you a future and a hope....And you will seek Me and find Me, when you search for Me with all your heart. I will be found by you, says the Lord..." Jeremiah 29:11-14.

As Job was going through his tribulation, he wrote: "But He knows the way that I take; when He has tested me, I shall come forth as gold" Job 23:10.

"The Lord is good, a stronghold in the day of trouble; and He knows those who trust in Him" Nahum 1:7.

~New Testament Words from God

"If God be for us, who can be against us?" Romans 8:31.

"The effectual fervent prayer of a righteous man avails much" James 5:16.

"Greater is He that is within you than he that is in the world" 1 John 4:4.

"I can do all things through Christ who strengthens me" Philippians 4:13.

"Be anxious for nothing, but in everything by prayer and supplication with thanksgiving, let your requests be made known to God; and the peace of God, which surpasses all understanding, will guard your hearts and minds through Christ Jesus" Philippians 4:6-7.

"I pray that out of his glorious riches he may strengthen you with power through his Spirit in your inner being" Ephesians 3:16.

"For by Him all things were created that are in heaven and that are on earth, visible and invisible, whether thrones or dominions or principalities or powers. All things were created through Him and for Him. And He is before all things, and in Him all things consist" Colossians 1:16-17.

~Paul wrote to the churches of his day, as well as our day:

"Be anxious for nothing, but in everything by prayer and supplication, with thanksgiving, let your requests be made known to God, and the peace of God, which surpasses all understanding, will guard your hearts and minds through Christ Jesus" Philippians 4:6-7

"Finally, brethren [and sisters], whatever things are true, whatever things are noble, whatever things are just, whatever things are pure, whatever things are lovely, whatever things are of good report, if there is any virtue and if there is anything praiseworthy – meditate on these things. The things which you learned and received and heard and saw in me, these do, and the God of peace will be with you" Philippians 4:8-9.

God's servant Paul wrote these words to the believers in the church at Thessalonica – and to us as well: *"Therefore brethren [and sisters], stand fast and hold the traditions which you were taught, whether by word or our epistle. Now may our Lord Jesus Christ Himself, and our God and Father, who has loved us and given us everlasting consolation and good hope by grace, comfort your hearts and establish you in every good word and work"* 2 Thessalonians 2:15-17.

"Now to the King eternal, immortal, invisible, to God who alone is wise, be honor and glory forever and ever. Amen" 1 Timothy 1:17

SONGS IN THE NIGHT

"Oh, sing to the Lord a new song! Sing to the Lord, all the earth. Sing to the Lord, bless His name; proclaim the good news of His Salvation from day to day" Psalm 96:1-2

Music will often touch my heart quicker than the spoken word. Feelings of praise and sorrow and inspiration are stirred by chords of music in an almost mysterious way. I've been uplifted by many songs and I'd like to share the titles of some of these songs in hopes that you might have an opportunity to be blessed by their music as well.

Below are some suggestions for songs that might encourage your heart. There are many great songs out there, but I've chosen some titles that go along with the messages of this book. These are a few of my favorites.

My original intent was to include at least a few lines from each song to whet your appetite to listen to the music for yourself, but copyright laws are so stringent I realized I would have to be content with giving you the title and performer. Their titles alone offer messages of hope. I pray the messages of these songs will bless your heart as much as they have mine.

--*"I Can Just Be Me"* – by Laura Story
--*"Blessings"* – by Laura Story
--*"A Way to See in the Dark"* – by Jason Gray
--*"There's No Thief Like Fear"* – by Jason Gray
--*"Change in the Making"* – by Addison Road
--*"I Can't Live a Day without You"* – by Avalon
--*"There You Were"* – by Avalon
--*"Indescribable"* – by Chris Tomlin
--*"Praise You in this Storm"* – by Casting Crowns
--*"Who Am I?"* -- by Casting Crowns
--*"Always Enough"* – by Casting Crowns
--*"Forgive Me"* – by Rebecca St. James
--*"Everytime I Breathe"* – by Big Daddy Weave

--"*My God's Enough*" – by Barlow Girls
--"*You Are God Alone*" – Phillips, Craig & Deane
--"*Jesus Take the Wheel*" – Carrie Underwood
--"*Find us Faithful*" – Steve Greene

*"He has put a new song in my mouth – praise to God;
Many will see it and fear, and will trust in the Lord"* Psalm 40:3

About the Author
Sandra Julian Barker

Here I am with a cupcake in my hand – one of my favorite things.
    I've written a number of novels and this is my first non-fiction, inspirational book – I hope it will not be the last. I've been a Christian since I was eight years old and I've been seeking to learn of Him for much of my life. God has been so good to me and my greatest desire is to bring honor and glory to His name through the talents He has given to me. If you have gleaned anything from this book -- all praise goes to King Jesus.

if you have an opportunity, check out my blog: www.sandra-ramblingrose.blogspot.com. I would love it if you would sign up to receive the weekly inspirational posts.

Also, if this book has blessed you in any way, please write a positive review on Amazon.com. Thank you!

-Photo: my husband Larry snapped this in front of a cupcake shop in Nevada. LNB

Made in the USA
Columbia, SC
23 March 2021